Advance praise fo

"*Spiritual Rebel* makes discoverin ap-
proach, Sarah's wisdom, wit, and knowledge take us on an illuminating
journey of discovery. A must-read for anyone seeking to find or deepen
their spiritual path."

—Francesco Mastalia, author of *Yoga: The Secret of Life*

"*Spiritual Rebel* is a fresh and timely take on religion and spirituality, particularly appealing to those who have outgrown more traditional ap-
proaches to 'finding God.' Sarah Bowen is a remarkably engaging writer,
using pop culture references in an inviting, highly personal approach that
from the first page invites you to join her in the exploration of the diverse teachings that many of the world's religions and spiritual teachers
provide. She weaves together the parallels and archetypal characteristics of these teachings that are both provocative and sensible, appealing
to the deepest sense of one's involvement and participation in the Great
Mystery. I highly recommend this for anyone who is exploring new ave-
nues for their spiritual discoveries."

—Dr. Steven Farmer, author of several best-selling books and oracle cards,
including *Animal Spirit Guides* and *Healing Ancestral Karma*

"Part interfaith instigator, part spiritual sister, Sarah Bowen will kindly and
impishly guide you to the next step of your journey to your own true heart."

—Barbara Becker, blogger *All Beings Everywhere*

"Sarah Bowen's *Spiritual Rebel* is a Jedi-infused, interspiritual smorgasbord of personal/universally attuned stories and activities that can be
tried out, tossed out, worked through, and which will awaken and encourage the depth and breadth of ourselves to flourish, even in the chaos
of our times. Approachable, a little snarky, a little sweet, Sarah brings us
along on a great journey of larger-Self discovery!"

—Leslie Reambeault, LCSW, eco-spiritual psychotherapist and author
of the forthcoming *Meeting Death: Mapping the Territory
for Therapists and Spiritual Companions*

"*Spiritual Rebel* will become a must-read. Sarah's experience with her religious heritage and her spiritual path will resonate with so many who, like
me, have experienced religious trauma and yet still yearn for a deeper
connection. The daily practices are practical, powerful, and enlightening.
Sarah has a gift of writing, is a gift in spirit, and this book is sacred."

—Rev. Karla Kamstra, owner and founder of The Bridge Spiritual Center

"Sarah is a skillful writer who weaves her spiritual knowledge throughout this book while providing simple and practical advice on ways to deepen your own personal spiritual journey. You will want to keep this book within arm's reach so that you can refer to it often."

–Reverend Joie Barry, founder of The Gathering of One

"With humor, wit, and authenticity Sarah Bowen provides a simple and easy roadmap for strengthening your spiritual muscles and living with a greater sense of wonder, freedom, and satisfaction."

–Bianca Lynn, transformational workshop leader and contributing author to the bestselling 365 Book Series

"In sum, I found *Spiritual Rebel* to be a humorous, slightly irreverent, concise guide for people who are searching for meaning—and aren't we all?"

–Judy Ranniger-Meza, LCSW

"With humor, occasional irreverence, and wisdom from life and study, Sarah Bowen offers an excellent book for the Spiritual-but-not-Religious person to explore and deepen what exactly that means to them personally. Through a series of very approachable and effective exercises, her readers are challenged to look at their preconceptions and their experiences to determine what being a spiritual rebel means for them—and how to use this new understanding to define their path in a way that is personally authentic and effective."

–AnnE O'Neil, author of *If You Want the Rainbow, Welcome the Rain: A Memoir of Grief and Recovery*

"*Spiritual Rebel* is a practical guide for personal growth and spiritual evolution. Those new to spirituality will find Sarah's casual, honest communication inspiring. Likewise, those who have been spiritual rebels for a long time will discover (or rediscover) ways to grow deeper into God and Spirit. *Spiritual Rebel* reminded me to appreciate my personal rebellion and embrace it as a valuable part of my own spiritual growth. May you find peace and friendship in these pages, fellow rebel. Welcome to the sangha."

–Rev. Nicole Losie, founder of Presence Yoga

"Sarah Bowen is a bookworm who can't stop reading, an unrelenting researcher, and a humble, nerdy rebel. As a result, *Spiritual Rebel* is an overflowing treasure trove of practices and resources that will inspire the Force within you."

–Sandy Fischman, interfaith/interspiritual minister

"Sarah Bowen writes in bold prose with vivid imagery compliments of precise vocabulary. Her tongue-in-cheek style conveys humor and an upbeat colloquial tone, which draws the reader into friendly intimacy, while her spicy language preserves her reputation as a spiritual rebel."

–Reverend Cheryl Trenholme, founder of One World Family

SPIRITUAL
REBEL

A POSITIVELY ADDICTIVE GUIDE TO FINDING
DEEPER PERSPECTIVE & HIGHER PURPOSE

SARAH BOWEN

Monkfish Book Publishing Company
Rhinebeck, New York

Paperback ISBN 978-1-948626-04-0
eBook ISBN 978-1-948626-05-7

Library of Congress Cataloging-in-Publication Data

Names: Bowen, Sarah, 1971- author.
Title: Spiritual rebel : a positively addictive guide to finding deeper
   perspective & higher purpose / Sarah Bowen.
Description: Rhinebeck, N.Y. : Monkfish Book Publishing Company, [2019]
Identifiers: LCCN 2019004966 (print) | LCCN 2019014493 (ebook) | ISBN
   9781948626057 (eBook) | ISBN 9781948626040 (pbk. : alk. paper)
Subjects: LCSH: Meaning (Philosophy) | Spirituality. | Spiritual life.
Classification: LCC B105.M4 (ebook) | LCC B105.M4 B68 2019 (print) | DDC
   204/.4--dc23
LC record available at https://lccn.loc.gov/2019004966

Monkfish Book Publishing Company
22 East Market Street, Suite 304
Rhinebeck, NY 12572
(845) 876-4861
monkfishpublishing.com

He's got to follow his own path.
No one can choose it for him.

PRINCESS LEIA

Contents

The F-word

It started with the F-word.
Not the highly-charged four-letter fuck.
Not the saintly five-letter faith.
It started with the Force.
Because in the beginning there was the word.

* * *

Or, in my case, the words. They appeared as gigantic yellow characters in all caps, rolling up a darkened movie theater screen. A wise sage named Obi-Wan Kenobi vividly described mystical energy called the Force. My life was forever changed.

Afterward, my imaginative friends and I met daily to act out stories about the Force, creating our own complex variants over time. With an unbridled spirit, we dubbed ourselves honorary members of the Rebel Alliance, standing bravely against any injustice or evil in our suburban neighborhood. We thought ourselves rare space warriors, yet we were unknowingly taking part in an age-old hero's journey which had been acted out for millennia. Inspired by the original Star Wars trilogy, we applied archetypal drama to our everyday lives on Earth.

Unsurprisingly, the myth of *Star Wars* felt more alive than what I learned at church. *Star Wars* had what my favorite Bible stories had—heroes, heroines, and wise sages. (Translation: Luke, Leia, and Yoda.) But unlike my church's religion, our *Star Wars* religiosity seemed more expansive and less exclusive. It was literally "Universe-al." Our neighborhood was a mashup of mostly Jewish and Catholic kids, with a few of us Protestants scattered around. Our families all had different religious beliefs and rituals, but there was one thing we kids could all agree on: the awesome power of the Force.

Looking back, I recognize that our youthful play was rife with sacred symbolism. Our memories of the film and the tales we created formed our oral tradition. Brightly colored Star Wars comic books became authoritative texts to consult during disagreements in our forming doctrine. As we acted out the myth, day after day, our play took on a ritualistic feel. Before long, the Kenner toy company hooked us on 3.75-inch-scale "icons" of our favorite characters. Cosmic sacred music blared from our tiny record players, compliments of the prolific composer John Williams.

Brushing off parental criticism that we were embracing violence with our lightsaber battles, we banded together as Jedis for the breathtaking destruction of the Death Star. Through our play, we learned about personal responsibility and the difficulty of making moral decisions. Mastering our fear of the evil Darth Vader, we began to understand the concepts of forgiveness and redemption.

Through *Star Wars*, we were discovering what our religious institutions were trying to teach us. But instead of being told precisely what to believe, we were encouraged to let belief *awaken*. And for some of us, that awakening became a tiny piece of our spiritual DNA.

And then I lost it.

I blame puberty. But for many years, I blamed religion. In seventh grade, my fellow hormone-rich, self-absorbed friends and I were enrolled in something called "confirmation class." Once a week we were taught about what our church affirmed— and by extension what we were supposed to think too. At great length, I learned about our denomination's faith, traditions, and practices. My focus, meanwhile, was on the cute blond boy in the class, and whether he liked me. Or if he thought I was too tall. Or too short. As I worried incessantly about my looks and what other people thought about me, the strong, confident child inside me turned into a nervous gangly girl who felt ugly, poor, and not good enough. Unable to connect the confirmation class teacher's lessons with anything relevant to my life, I began to harbor a deep, dark secret that I could not share: *I did not believe.*

As a preacher's kid, this was quite a liability. Somehow though, I managed to pass the class final (including writing an ordered list, pulled from my shaky memory, of all the books of the Bible) so that I could stand in front of the entire church congregation and be confirmed—right next to that cute blond boy. While my father was always willing to help me with any questions, and never told me what to believe, my self-absorption was growing to a colossal size.

Eventually, my secret attracted friends. Their names were Guilt and Depression. Soon, they found a leader. Her name was Addiction. Slyly, I hid them all behind studded black leather, blue hair, and absurd amounts of black eyeliner. Increasingly, my weekends were rife with the proverbial sex, drugs, and rock 'n roll. Or in my 1980s version, 40-oz. bottles of cheap beer, cartons of Camels, long nights full of punk rock, and random awkward hookups in the backseat of my tiny Ford Fiesta.

I got so good at all that, I figured I'd try it for another four years through college.

Occasionally, I attended my father's church out of loyalty to him. But my late Saturday bar nights soon turned that into rarely. It became harder to ignore the exclusionary beliefs of some church members, which left me constantly gnashing my teeth. Confused by their words and actions, which seemed inconsistent with my experience of this "God" thing, I slowly drifted away from attending church at all. My life and academics suffered as I struggled to deal with anxiety and trauma, without the support of a community or spiritual path.

I oozed resistance with a side of defiance, some refusal, and a healthy dose of stubbornness. More and more, I spent time rebelling against, well, everything. Railing about what I was against, I spent very little time talking about what I was *for*. Religion was one of my favorite targets. Time after time, I would point out what was wrong with this group or that ritual. This dogma or that congregation. This religious leader or that scripture.

I became a rebel without a real cause, stuck in a place of dividedness. My only cause was knocking down yours—making you out to be an "other" who was just plain wrong. With this narrow-minded tunnel vision, I spoke in gross generalizations: "Religion is the opium of the people!" I'd insist, quoting Karl Marx, or "Religion is for the weak-minded!" That was me in the corner, losing my religion.

Graduating from college to pursue a life in New York City was the final nail in the coffin. Consequently, I became a very successful workaholic, seeking sanity through money. As I tried to avoid the flaws of this plan, my apartment became littered with self-help books. Convinced that the key to balance was in the next book, I tried to fill the hole created from turning my back on spirituality. Over the next 10 years, my apartments and jobs improved. Traveling extensively on business and vacationing in foreign countries, my passport proved I could get around. Stockpiling stuff, chasing success, and wooing money, everything appeared to be going as planned. Yet I was drowning in addiction, and a fathomless void was growing inside.

Too many mornings I woke up next to my friend Guilt. Occasionally, it was a threesome with Shame. Lust, Greed, and Gluttony had assuredly been present the prior night. In my hungover state, Sloth would keep me company. The Seven Deadly Sins had moved into my Hell's Kitchen apartment with me and my not-so-secret secrets.

One day I received a call from my sister, asking me to come to the hospital ASAP. Mom and Dad had just returned from vacation, and my father was sick. An excruciating six weeks later, his body gave out. The day he died, I woke up hungover and dressed for battle: black steel-toe boots, ripped jeans, and a Superman T-shirt. As I walked across the city to the hospital, I passed a group of schoolchildren. A small boy pointed at me and declared, "Superman!" A little girl looked at him with disdain and corrected, "Super*girl*!"

But I had never felt less super.

When I arrived at the hospital, our family held hands in a circle. Someone said a prayer. My mind screamed, "Need to get out of here!" Forcefully, I stormed through the hospital's huge glass doors and marched up First Avenue with no other direction in mind than *away*, which happened to be north. Angry, with tears streaming down my face, I stomped along, helpless and hopeless.

Twenty blocks later, I spotted a chapel across the street. I remembered all the times my father had been called away for an emergency at the church. Or the hospital. Or the nursing home. I decided now was my emergency. I tried the doors. Locked.

Angrier, I continued up the street, soon spotting a synagogue. Locked. A cathedral. Locked. Finally, I saw a church with the doors open. I burst in, yelling, "I need clergy!" Softly, the janitor told me to wait in a pew. Soon, a man appeared and sat down in front of me. He gently asked me what was going on.

Out spouted my anger at God. "Why would he take his best employee? It's not fair! It's too soon! He's only 65. I didn't get to say goodbye right!" That was the gist of my 20-minute rant.

"Do you have a Bible?" the minister asked. I looked at him blankly. Really? What good would a Bible do me now? My father was dead. Hadn't this man heard me?

As he handed me one to take home, I somehow muttered, "Thanks," and left quickly. I apparently was not going to get the answers I desperately wanted. Walking further north to Central Park, I sat with my unwanted gift on the grass. I don't remember how long I sat there, but somehow, eventually, I made it back to my apartment.

I remember feeling numb.

The void I ignored for years was now a gigantic abyss. As an addict, I knew how to deal with that numbness. And it worked. Or so I thought. Until it didn't.

Raw and lonely, I felt separated from others, drowning in grief. Even functioning felt impossible. It's hard to keep everything together when you are hollow inside. Soon, Lyme disease reared its ugly head—a curse that began to ravage my body—as addiction continued its work on my mind.

Eventually, I decided life had become unmanageable. At the end of my rope, I sought help. Doctors, massage therapists, and a kick-ass acupuncturist helped reduce my pain level as well as increase my stamina. With the help of strangers, I started a spiritual recovery. The Seven Deadlies were evicted without notice. I experienced the power of 12-step fellowship. And, finally, I began to look deeply into religious questions.

Because the word *God* kept coming up. And I felt about God a bit like I did about Darth Vader. So as a self-identified nerd,

I headed to my favorite religious institution: the library. After months of pouring over books about the world's great spiritual traditions, I got myself all twisted up. Eventually, my friend Dianne asked me directly, "Hey, Sarah, can you make trees?"

I looked at her as if she had three heads and replied, "Of course not." Her answer—"Well, someone or something can"—gave me the foundation for a workable spirituality. I realized that nailing down precisely what I believed wasn't the point. I just needed to understand there was a Force working in the world—and it wasn't me alone. The seeker's path started to unfold in front of me, step by small step. Soon, I became positively addicted to spirituality.

And here's where the story gets unusually *freaky*.

Somehow I found myself enrolled in what I coyly refer to as Serenity School. Of course, it's not called Serenity School by the people who founded it. Instead, it's described as an interfaith seminary. But when I say the word *seminary* to people, they often roll their eyes and get a glazed-over look. Suddenly, they're playing videos in their head of everything they hate about religion, and inserting me into scenes. Let me assure you that I did not go to a school like *that*.*

Instead, I spent time in a community of wildly diverse students from innumerable paths: from an Ifa priestess who did amazing blessings over water, to an Orthodox Jewish woman who refrained from holding the microphone on Saturdays (and requested the song "Jesus Freak" for our graduation party). There were more than a few Christians. And to my delight, I also met Pagans, Wiccans, Humanists, agnostics, and more than one atheist. In the classroom I uncovered a boatload of other recovering addicts as well as a handful of massage therapists, lightworkers, talented intuitives, and yoga teachers. My academic advisor was a Sufi. It would be an understatement to say it blew my mind.

In the One Spirit Interfaith Seminary program, founder Diane Berke and the diverse staff gently encouraged me to embrace *all* religious paths as valid and worthy of exploration. Instead of subscribing to any specific dogma or creed, we were asked simply to agree to a community code of ethics. Some of us were entrenched in a specific path already, but many of us were free agents who were in for quite a ride. My classmate Shelly observed, "It's a good thing that our eyes open slowly. Otherwise, our heads would blow off."

Together, my class spent month after month learning each other's spiritual traditions as well as some new ones I had never heard of. Digging in, I began to jettison some of the bullshit I had clung to about religion. First, I realized it was okay to question what I had been taught: A spiritual path is about asking questions, not seeking certainty through answers. Next, I embraced the meditative, contemplative, and mystical experiences that are at the heart of what we call *interspirituality*.** As the program continued, new roomies appeared at my apartment: Meaning, Purpose, Kindness, Courage, and Authenticity. Grudgingly, I let in Forgiveness, Equanimity, and Love. (Admittedly, they might even be our best housemates.) Gratefully, I tossed out most of my fossil-filled baggage to make room for everyone.

Uncovering wisdom in each new sacred text, I glimpsed the archetypes behind my childhood heroes. Soon my bookshelves overflowed with cosmic and earthly words: Yogananda and Zukav were now placed after Yoda.***

In every activity, I looked for a sacred angle. In every conversation, I swapped spiritual aha! moments. Narrowly escaping that lightspeed crash fueled by illness, stress, addiction, and overwork, I reached back to a belief in the Force to recover my hope.

Now I'm a fierce advocate for Hope. I suppose I was from childhood, fueled by the tiny holographic Princess Leia pleading, "Help me Obi-Wan Kenobi, you're my only hope." Since then, the word has burrowed deep into my heart, but my pain made it hard to access and I became hopeless. But I have recovered it, inspired by my childhood princess—or more accurately the human behind her, Carrie Fisher. When I was six, Leia taught me I could grow up to run as fast as and fight as hard as any boy—even when wearing a dress. As I aged, my connection to the woman behind the role grew: first as I battled addiction, and then as I fought the stigma attached to depression and hypomania (which I refer to as having occasional strong fluctuations in my Force). Through Carrie, what's known as the divine feminine appeared, encouraging me to finally voice my sexual identity (i.e., I had a crush on both Han Solo *and* Leia). At Carrie's death in late 2016, my higher purpose showed itself: To be a tireless advocate for the hope that our spiritual and religious beliefs need not separate us, but can offer us richer, more diverse connections and community.

So throughout this book, I offer you my services as an interspiritual tour guide. Even though each of us must discover our own path, and no one can choose it for us, I do have some imaginative ideas you might like to try out on your journey. As a result, this book is not an instruction manual with perfect directions to enlightenment. It does not suggest adherence to any specific belief system. Nor is it a scholarly treatise on the optimal way to reach Nirvana. You will never hear me claim that one belief system is better than another, or that any practice is more sacred than any other.

Instead, *Spiritual Rebel* is a field guide for exploring *your* spirituality. Through its pages, you will be invited to clarify the beliefs that are personally meaningful to you and to redefine outdated concepts to which you might be clinging. You'll also have the opportunity to explore creative mix-and-match practices, along with some new ways to experience connection. Above all else, you'll be encouraged to express your unique style of spiritual freedom.

NOTES

* *Seminary* owes its heritage to the Latin word *seminarium*, which means plant nursery or, more metaphorically, breeding grounds, where attendees are being grown into their roles, so to speak. *Serenity* derives from the Latin *serēnus*, meaning clear or unclouded sky (or mind, in my case).

** The word *interspirituality* was coined by spiritual teacher Wayne Teasdale. Describing a spiritual perspective rather than a specific path, interspirituality recognizes that beneath theological beliefs and rituals there is a deeper, shared unity of experience underlying them all: the common values of peace, compassionate service, and love for all of creation. By bringing an open mind, generous spirit, and warm heart to our search, we can find expression through myriad wisdom traditions. Interspirituality's roots draw from a wide range of teachings, including those by Baha'u'llah (founder of the Bahá'í faith), Indian mystic Ramakrishna, Trappist monk Thomas Merton, and Father Bede Griffiths, among others. Interspirituality shares many ideas with perennialism and universalism.

*** Indian yogi, guru, and author Paramahansa Yogananda introduced Kriya Yoga (an Eastern spirituality based on breathwork, mantras, and meditation) to the U.S. starting in the 1920s. Founding the Self-Realization Fellowship, he first spread the tradition along the West Coast. His wildly popular 1946 book *Autobiography of a Yogi* has sold over four million copies. Anecdotally, I feel compelled to add that Apple Inc. cofounder Steve Jobs reread it annually. Self-realization states that we already possess an inner knowing of who we are and of God. The key is direct experience (through meditation) rather than the learning of beliefs.

Gary Zukav's first book, *The Dancing Wu Li Masters: An Overview of the New Physics*, is a stellar example of how science and spirituality are not in opposition. Ten years later, in 1989, he wrote his No. 1 *New York Times* bestseller *The Seat of the Soul*. It stayed on the list for three years. It's Oprah's favorite book (other than the Bible, she claims). Underlying Zukav's books is the philosophy that power comes from within, not bestowed from outside. Further, for each of us to cultivate our authentic power, we must develop our emotional awareness, hone our intuition, make responsible choices, and trust in the Universe.

Are you a spiritual rebel?

If you've read this far, I'm 99.99 percent sure you are.
But it can't hurt to check.

* * *

Defining spiritual rebel is a bit like describing the rules of Fight Club. The first rule of Fight Club is you do not talk about Fight Club. Similarly, many of us have hidden our rebelliousness at one point or another: You do not speak about spirituality—and don't even think about voicing the word *religion.* (If you are among the lucky ones who have been freely verbose since you popped out of the womb, keep reading anyway.) *Apostate. Heretic. Dissident. Divergent. Rabble Rouser. Inciter. Instigator. Troublemaker.* Some of us have heard those words, and not in the kindest tones. Others have been pummeled with the word *Unbeliever.* More than a few of us have experienced the pain of being pushed out of a community they once felt loved by when the edges of their beliefs started to expand. As a result, we can be cautious about belief statements or creeds, preferring a do-it-yourself attitude towards our spirituality.

According to a 2018 Pew Research Center study, only 39 percent of U.S. adults consider themselves "highly religious."

Until recently, Pew (and other folks) categorized those of us who couldn't neatly check a box for a mainstream religion into categories like *none, nothing in particular,* or *unaffiliated.* Yet the researchers were missing a key point: Many who didn't fit easily into the surveys were becoming increasingly spiritual. Our definition of religion is expanding. We're looking for new ways of connecting—with a deeper perspective and a higher purpose. We're redefining what *sacred, spiritual,* and *religious* mean for us. Drawing on activities that come from multiple faith traditions, we may do yoga in the morning, meditate in the afternoon, hit a popup Shabbat some Friday nights, gather in community the following Sunday morning, and teach our kids about the awesome power of the Cosmos. We may spend summer weekends roaming through festivals, and we most likely resist being tied to any particular building or specific location. We're as likely to say *May the odds be ever in your favor* or *May the Force be with you* or *Namaste* as we are to say goodbye; our language is increasingly fluid and multicultural rather than tied to a rigid formula. Of course, some of us may do none of these things, practicing a spiritual path that is undefinable—even to us. Or we may be part of something that's super meaningful to us, but which others criticize.

We are experiencing a significant period of spiritual freedom of choice. Postmodern spiritual paths, fueled by our growing technological connections, appear from near and far—including seemingly odd places.

In 2001, more than 70,000 people embraced the Force of *Star Wars,* identifying religiously as Jedi in a census taken by the Australian Board of Statistics. Another 390,127 Jedi showed up on the U.K.'s 2001 census. While there has been some speculation on how many of these census takers are answering "seriously," the 2017 documentary *American Jedi* shines a light on just how real Jediism can be for some of its followers, chronicling three people using the path to heal the emotional wounds of rape, marital infidelity, and youthful indiscretions. Going beyond sheer fandom, these members of an American Jedi Order are incredibly serious about their practice of an applied religious philosophy inspired by *Star Wars*. While many people may not consider their mythology to be on par with the Buddha, Krishna, Muhammad, or Jesus (or myriad other spiritual all-stars), a Jedi might ask people to dig further. The value of a myth is not in how true it is, but in how deeply one connects with it. And how it affects our lives.

Likewise, Jediism isn't the only spiritual path that has its roots in modern film and fiction. Two graduates from Harvard Divinity School, Casper ter Kuile and Vanessa Zoltan, made headlines in 2017 when their podcast "Harry Potter and the Sacred Text" catapulted up the iTunes chart to the No. 2 podcast in America. It's now a robust program with satellite groups, live shows, and pilgrimages. Exploring central themes through the book characters and story, Casper, Vanessa, and their growing team engage in traditional forms of sacred reading seeking to unearth the hidden gifts within "even the most mundane sentences." Underlying the program is a simple probing question: *What if we read the books we love as if they were sacred texts?* And just like that, the third-century Christian practice of *Lectio Divina* has been modernized.

But let's not stop there. The Church of the Latter-Day Dude, a self-described "open-source religion," borrows heavily from Taoism and claims 450,000 Dudeist priests worldwide. Followers can glean wisdom from *The Dude De Ching*, a modern translation of *The Tao Te Ching*. Based on the age-old wisdom of Lao Tzu, it is supported by quotes from the movie *The Big Lebowski*.

Whether these movements are "valid" religions or pure absurdity isn't the question. Although spiritual rebels hold strongly to our individuality, these alternative spiritual communities are flourishing. Operating outside traditional religious institutions, they still have something in common with how religions originally evolved: the search for meaning with the support of a community.

For many of us, that search is sparked after doing self-work and self-care. Not surprisingly, the wellness market is growing in leaps and bounds. According to the Global Wellness Institute, the world now spends $3.7 trillion a year. From wellness tourism and spa visits, to healthy eating, fitness, and weight loss, we collectively spend oodles of money. On ourselves.

After we commit to our own wellness, deepening our perspective can lead to impactful choices that ripple out beyond our individual lives. Increasingly, I've found that looking at each decision in my life through a spiritual lens means my search for meaning succeeds in going beyond self-centeredness.

How I spend my money matters: From choosing a This Bar Saves Lives snack bar with my tea, to donating a portion of this book's proceeds to charity:water, small changes that rebel against my "normal" way of consuming and handling money can go a long way in connecting me to others and to something greater than myself.

And how I allocate my time is important: Is *my* time all about *me*? Or am I engaging in actions that help sustain people, the planet, and its creatures? Do I support my friends with depth or am I just mindlessly clicking likes and dropping emojis on my social feeds? Does my spirituality extend beyond seeking my own blissful highs to helping those drowning in devastating lows? Because if I constrain my spirituality to being about me, I rob us all of the richness we can experience when united for a higher purpose. Wellness means *I am okay*. Spirituality leads to *We are okay*.

This is not a guilt trip. We need both. And we need each other. So come, all you who are spiritual-but-not-religious, solidly secular, spiritual innovators, heathens, spiritually woke, religion resisters, spiritual-but-not-affiliated, pagans, agnostics, 12-steppers, comfortably communitied, and diversely devout. And of course, you Jedis, Dudeists, Potterheads, and wellness buffs, too. You belong.

Whether you were raised atheist, rejected the religion of your birth, fell deeply in love with the spiritual path of your neighbor, or reframed and reclaimed the sacred through new perspectives, we have a place for you, too. Because if you resist being pigeon-holed, limited, or even defined, you are indeed spiritually rebellious.

Although we each may tread a unique and profoundly personal path, if you reject what does not feel authentic to your own experience of spirituality, you are decidedly a spiritual rebel.

A unicorn among sheep

All the beasts obeyed Noah
when he admitted them to the ark.
All but the unicorn.
Confident of its strength,
the unicorn boasted,
"I shall swim."

UKRANIAN FOLKTALE

* * *

My eight-year-old friend Teddy is a spunky, pint-sized example of an emerging spiritual rebel. She and her classmates were
given whiteboards to explore what they wanted to do in their
futures. Sadly, *I want to be rich* and *I want to be a pop star* were
the prevalent wishes. But not for Teddy. Her response? *I will
discover a unicorn.*

I had to bite my tongue to keep from offering to help her set
up a GoFundMe account for the endeavor. Just what is it about
these magical creatures that captures our collective imagi-
nation? From references in the ancient Hebrew scriptures to
the cool million John D. Rockefeller Jr. paid for the medieval
Unicorn Tapestries to the trendy Unstable Unicorns strategic

card game, we have been fascinated with unicorns since the Bronze Age.

Rare, wild, and full of potential, this creature exists gracefully just barely beyond human sight. Often appearing in stories to guide humans at critical junctures, their backs never see human riders or, God forbid, a saddle. And so it occurs to me that the unicorn may be our postmodern version of glimpsing the divine. We want to believe in the unseen, the untouchable, the mystical. Desiring so strongly to be unique, we adopt the unicorn as our exclusive luxe icon, fearing being demoted to something ordinary.

Like a sheep.

Sheepish. Being fleeced. One of the Sheeple. We've given sheep a bad rap, relegating them to derogatory slurs as an example of unwanted conformity. Their lives are commonly undervalued—they are mere animals to be used for food and fashion, based on our beliefs about what a sheep is for.

But beliefs are not facts. They help us navigate our world, but do not have to be fixed, unchanging. Which is lucky for us, because sometimes these ideas help us; other times, they can limit us. For example, let's reconsider sheep. Due to amazing memory capability, sheep can remember at least 50 different other sheep and humans for many years, and even recognize emotions through facial expressions. Extremely intelligent, they can solve complex problems, with IQs nearly as high as the notoriously clever pig. Skilled herbalists, some sheep will self-medicate illnesses by seeking out specific plants that can alleviate their symptoms. Sacred to Egyptians, many sheep were mummified with the same care as humans.

Quickly, new information begets altered beliefs and helps us toss out biases. While visiting South Africa, my opinions about sheep did a 180 when I met a remarkable Thaba Manzi Pedi sheep named Lammie. Dwelling at the Hoedspruit Endangered Species Centre, Lammie is a surrogate mother for many of the wildlife sanctuary's orphaned baby rhinos whose parents have been killed by poachers. Comforting, playing with, and guiding the colossal animals, Lammie is clearly a valued and respected member of both the family of rhinos and the center's staff. (One might even say she's lovingly raising chubby unicorns?)

Now go back and take a closer look at the cover of this book, specifically at that fuzzy yellow dude you probably thought was a unicorn. I call him Unifred. (I call everything I name some version of Fred. I have no idea why.) I suppose you could label him a sheepicorn or unisheep. (My friend Steve calls him a wooly unicorn.) Ultimately, it doesn't matter. Because the label is not the point: The process is the point. For me, this zany mythical creature embodies the best qualities of both unicorn and sheep. He's a symbol for what happens when I bust my biases, and he's ever reminding me I don't have to slur anyone to build myself up as unique. I can hold fast to my individuality while still being in community.

What happens if we apply this concept to our spirituality?

Sex scandals, power plays, and the political co-opting of religion have turned many of us away from the religious institutions of our youth. Hurtful statements that God was anti-this, anti-that, or even anti-us may have sunk in and festered. Or we just may have misunderstood what was being presented to us as we tried to process complex concepts before we were old enough to comprehend abstract thoughts. Sometimes the narrative, or story, of the religion we were taught fell flat for us in the modern age—we were unable to feel the story as our own or connect with it. Others of us grew up without any knowledge about religion or spirituality, except for what we saw on the news or the stories we heard from our friends' painful experiences.

And so we inherited—and often created—beliefs about what spirituality and religion meant. As spiritual rebels, we can relook at these beliefs to see if they should be held or adapted based on new information and experiences. As spiritual rebels, we can reject things that don't work for us, yet still allow others the autonomy to believe what is meaningful to them. During our redefining process, it's important to clarify our own beliefs rather than to just stand in opposition to what we don't believe in.

I'd like to go down the rabbit hole a bit on this, using one of my favorite renegades: Richard Buckminster Fuller. I fell in love with him the first time I set foot in a geodesic dome. As an architect, Bucky popularized that innovative design. He was a true nonconformist—so much so that he was expelled from Harvard. Twice. He struggled with alcohol and depression, and even attempted suicide.

Yet Bucky was awarded 28 patents, authored more than 30 books, served as the world president of Mensa (the elite high-IQ society) for almost a decade, and received the Presidential Medal of Freedom. His futurist philosophy would go on to influence 20th-century design, fuel the sustainability movement, invigorate energy-efficient housing, and shake up linguists. The Buckminster Fuller Institute refers to him posthumously as a "comprehensive anticipatory design scientist."

So what happened?

Recalling his turnaround later in life, Bucky described being on the verge of committing suicide in Lake Michigan, when he heard the following, as Jonathon Keats recounts in *You Belong to the Universe: Buckminster Fuller and the Future*:

You do not have the right to eliminate yourself. You do not belong to you. You belong to Universe. Your significance will remain forever obscure to you, but you may assume that you are fulfilling your role if you apply yourself to converting your experiences to the highest advantage of others.

Whether this was "Universe," Bucky's true self, God, or some other voice isn't the key point here. What's most significant is the effect on Bucky's life. He had found a new perspective, leading him to a higher purpose. In the process, he would author this wise advice: "You never change things by fighting the existing reality. To change something build a new model that makes the existing model obsolete." I think Bucky hits on a paramount point here, so let's dissect it:

> You never change things by fighting the existing reality.

Yet this is what we rebels often do. We fight *against* what we don't like instead of working *for* the change we want to see. With the rise of social media, I see this type of behavior every day. My feeds are full of memes and quotes about what people hate, sound bites about what they are against. But when I ask for more information about what someone is for, often they answer with a version of: "I'm for the cessation of what I'm against." So let's go back to Bucky's quote:

> To change something build a new model that makes the existing model obsolete.

Let me be clear that I'm not advocating for religion to become obsolete. Far from it. People have a right to their own opinions and perspectives on religion; that's our First Amendment in action: "Congress shall make no law respecting an establishment of religion or prohibiting the free exercise thereof." This is what the rebellious early Americans sought, and current generations work hard to maintain. What I am advocating is for us to keep building our own personal spiritual models that make any existing model of how we were living without spirituality obsolete.

Shel Silverstein's book *The Missing Piece Meets the Big O* makes this point in a mere 519 words. Unable to move due to its shape, a triangle-shaped "missing piece" searches for another piece to complete it and take it somewhere. But each attempted pairing doesn't fit properly. It tries changing itself in numerous ways to attract the "right piece." Finally, after some time, the missing piece finds a Pac-man shaped piece that works, at least until the missing piece begins to grow and outgrows its newfound friend. Again, the missing piece is on its own. Before long, it meets a circle named the Big O and becomes hopeful for a match. Yet the Big O declares it is complete on its own and advises that the missing piece could be complete on its own as well.

The missing piece must build a new model. It must realize that it already has everything it needs; the model of incompleteness is obsolete. Being triangular, it just needs to start rolling to wear off its sharp corners. Then it will be a rolling whole. Like the missing piece, we need to wear off our sharp corners. We need to toss out the perspectives that no longer work for us.

We need to throw out our sacred trash.

Taking out the sacred trash

It filled the can, it covered the floor,
It cracked the window and blocked the door.

SHEL SILVERSTEIN

* * *

Admittedly, releasing long-held beliefs is not always an easy task. Some of us have been threatened with some pretty horrible consequences if we think for ourselves. Others of us may have intermingled our principles and personality to such an extent that we worry without them, "Who will I be?" A friend once described the process to me as, "My insides are being rearranged."

Letting go can be uncomfortable. Spine-chillingly scary. Somberly sad. Disorienting. And at the same time, it can also be joyful and hair-raisingly exciting. Freeing. Relieving. Delightfully comforting. Embracing a both/and instead of either/or mindset, we can allow all these feelings to coexist.

Below, I offer a spiritual experiment for you to consider. As I waded into my own personal rubbish pile, I was surprised at the sheer volume of beliefs I had not reevaluated since my teens. For many, I was unable even to remember where the idea came from or who taught it to me. For others, I remembered with chest-tightening resentment just exactly who told me. Because I vehemently reject "Do as I say, not as I do," here is a peek into what I discovered.

I *do not* believe:

- That it isn't okay to question
- That not believing in all of the religious ideas my father did dishonors him in any way
- That pop culture myths are any less worthy of study than age-old spiritual ones
- That it's not okay to use the F-word in spiritual settings (though on challenging days I could use a language detox)
- That being spiritual means I am entitled to bash religions (or religious people)
- That there is a punishing divine figure doling out his vengeance whenever I am not being my best self
- That spirituality must always be quiet and serene
- That religion and science are opposites
- That business and spirituality are diametrically opposed
- That to be spiritual means I can't also be a consumer
- That prayer is only for Christians and meditation only for Buddhists
- That because I don't agree with all of the tenets of a religion, I have to throw it entirely away
- That if I become a member of one spiritual community, it means I cannot join others
- That by being part of any community, I have to believe exactly the same things as the other members
- That I must live in a particular country or be of a specific ethnicity to learn from the teachings of Krishna,

Buddha, Zoroaster, Moses, Jesus, Lao Tzu, Mahāvira, or myriad other wise ones

- That religion is for the weak
- That scandals by some religious people negate the entire religion or the compassionate work religious institutions do to help their communities
- That to justify my own spiritual path, I have to trash yours
- That *God* is the only valid name for the divine mystery
- That people who do use the word *God* are flawed and worthy of my ridicule
- That being born with alcoholic genes (and following them) makes me a sinner
- That identifying as bisexual means I am an abomination
- That I am fallen or unworthy
- That Jesus is the only way to God
- That there is only one path to anything
- And that wanting to embody the traits of a Jedi is somehow not "real spirituality"

Those statements were just the top layer of my litter. Pages and pages of words poured out of me, accompanied by a healthy dose of tears, anger, and F-words. My head throbbed, as if reeling from a substantial hangover. So I took a nap.

Many hours later, I woke up and tossed the entire notebook into the trash, committing to reject all those ideas I was told by others, or developed myself, that no longer felt true to me. Smiling like a Cheshire cat, I felt as relieved as if I had just completed the New York City marathon—or what I expect that might feel like. I am not nearly coordinated enough to run long distances without injuring myself.

It's true, our discrete sacred trash piles are likely to be vastly different. And some of my sacred trash may include beliefs that you hold meaningful. And vice versa. Yet our goals can be the same: to release what no longer supports us in order to build a new perspective that makes the old one obsolete. Taking out our trash can open up space within us. It clears the self-harming thoughts of *unworthy, fallen, sinful*. It makes space for self-caring states of *joy*, *serenity*, and *bliss*.

Of course, just like in your home, taking out the sacred trash is not a one-time event. It's a practice we can return to again and again, to refresh ourselves and our spirituality. I invite you to try to offload just a bit today.

SPIRITUAL EXPERIMENT #1:
TAKING OUT THE SACRED TRASH

I suspect that you, like me, may have a stack of unused or half-used notebooks sitting somewhere. Grab one. Not the one you don't want to part with, or the one that was a special gift. Find the one that looks a little beaten up, the one sitting forlornly at the bottom of the pile with no hopes of ever being used for your bestselling novel or doctoral thesis. If you don't have a stack, pop over to the nearest dollar store and grab the cheap one with the ding on the front, or the one someone marred with a footprint.

1. *Silence* your phone, computer, or anything around you that might ring, ding, or vibrate.
2. *Close your eyes and take a deep breath.* Exhale slowly.
3. *Open to the first page of your notebook and write these words at the top: Clinging to beliefs that no longer feel true robs me of spiritual freedom.*

4. *Close your eyes again and take another deep breath.* Exhale slowly.
5. *Ask yourself this question:* What spiritual or religious beliefs am I clinging to as "true" that do not feel "true"?
6. *Write the answer in your notebook.* Whether it is two words or two full pages, keep writing till the thought feels completely expressed.
7. *Close your eyes once more and take a deep breath.* Exhale slowly.
8. *Ask yourself:* And what else am I clinging to as "true" that does not feel "true"? What practices, actions, or rituals no longer feel nurturing or sustaining?
9. *Repeat steps 6 to 8* until you've got nothing else left to write.
10. *Ask yourself:* "Am I ready to consider letting go?" The key word here is *consider.* If you've held these convictions for a long time, you may feel slightly anxious. You may not be ready to let go. You may need to sit with your notebook and drink a hot cup of coffee. Or a walk around the block may ease your separation anxiety. Some people have told me that taking a nap helps. Take your time: minutes, hours, or days. Revisit the words and ask the questions again.
11. *When you hear yes, acknowledge the notebook.* Thank it for holding your words, your sacred trash. Thank the beliefs you're throwing away for helping you when they were necessary. Let them know it is time for you to move on.
12. *Put your sacred trash in the rubbish bin.* Yes, of course, you can use a shredder if yours is juicy.

For some of you, I suspect the word *God* might have popped up. That word regularly appears during this experiment, which makes sense. It's hard to talk about spirituality or religion without the G-word appearing.

As a spirituality writer, I find that the question I dread most (and perhaps consequently the one I am most often asked) is "Do you believe in God?" It's impossible for me to answer the question with a simple yes or no. For me, as for many of us, the G-word is a loaded one. Instead, I answer with a question, "What do you mean by the word *God*?"

Each answer to *that* query is different. People's descriptions of God are unique since their experiences are personal. But the lion's share of people I speak with (and, I'm assuming, most of you reading this book) do not believe in anything that looks like Santa's long-lost brother—some robed character with a white beard, seated on a throne, nestled gently in the clouds, judging our worthiness, and directing our lives with his superpowers. Nor do we believe or think that it/she/he is punishing us, like some sort of supernatural pissed-off parent figure. Yet these descriptions may abound in our memories of what "religious people" think of when *they* say God.

Relying on the almighty world of Google and Wikipedia for instant access to the answers to our questions, we may be frustrated that our technology can't come up with a single, solid answer either. *Hey, Siri, does God exist? Hey, Alexa, can you send me divine presence (with expedited shipping)? Google Maps, take me to the Source.* But, alas, our mighty technology can't resolve these queries.

And so some of us reject God.

But maybe, just maybe, our problem isn't with God—it is with our definition of God. During my search, I came across this great quote by the 17th-century Indian poet Tukaram:

"There is nothing in your life that will not change, especially your ideas of God."

Many of us aren't aware of the seemingly endless list of descriptions people use to describe the focus of their spirituality—whether it has a form or is formless. I certainly wasn't. I thought it was the G-way or the highway. As I started digging into my issues with the G-word, I discovered enormous diversity in the words people use to describe their experiences of immanence, transcendence, and the mystery that lies just beyond our grasp. (Which in hindsight makes sense. We are a species that relies on language to navigate our world. A big part of our human experience is naming things, which can be helpful, but also limiting because we each attach different meaning—and often baggage—to names. Like Unifred. Or Fredicorn. Or God.)

So I decided I needed even more information. Again, I consulted books about the world's great religions, philosophical movements, and spiritual traditions, thinking that if I could decide what system worked for me, then I'd know which interpretation or name would work.

Fortunately, I soon accepted nailing down the precise word or concept wasn't the point. I just needed to understand that the mysterious force working in the world wasn't my ego alone. This force could be described in innumerable ways, each of them adding a layer of curiosity to contemplate. Exploring each one like a single pixel in an immense photograph, when added together, each depiction deepened and expanded my spiritual view.

Refreshingly, not all were names or even nouns. Wellbeing advocate Deepak Chopra told me, "God is a process." Jewish philosopher Abraham Joshua Heschel put it like this: "God is light." Kabbalist David A. Cooper offered, "God is a verb." Mythologist Joseph Campbell said, "God is a symbol." Einstein professed, "God is cosmic." Rev. Ani suggested, "God is the flow of life." And Science Mike claimed, "God is the Initial Singularity of physics." In book after book, and podcast after podcast, I heard definitions of the G-word that sounded nothing like my definition of some cross between a vengeful parent, Santa Claus, Lord Voldemort, and Darth Vader.

More and more, I confirmed that no two people's definitions of God were the same. Further, I learned that the names for God were no different. They were words for the same concept—personal experiences that were described in the words of local languages by individual people. The word was not the thing. It was a pointer.

There's a Buddhist parable that explains this concept much better than I can:

> A Zen student had become troubled by the contradictions he saw in Buddhist doctrine and was seeking answers. His teacher invited the boy to join his evening walk with his dog.
>
> "You must understand," said the teacher, "words are only guideposts. Never let words or symbols get in the way of truth. Here, I'll show you."
>
> With that, the teacher called his happy dog to fetch a stick. The dog would run ahead, fetch the stick, and then run back. Then, wagging his tail, the dog would wait to fetch again.
>
> "Fetch me the moon," the teacher said to the dog, pointing to the full moon.
>
> "Where is my dog looking?" the teacher asked the student.
>
> "He's looking at your finger," replied the boy.
>
> "Exactly. Don't be like my dog. Don't confuse the pointing finger with the thing that is being pointed at. All our words are only guideposts. Every person fights their way through the words of others to find their own truth."

For example, my cats Deacon and Buba-ji are unlikely to describe themselves as cats. The word *cat* was invented by humans, it's not "what they are" or what they would call themselves. Likewise, I'm not sure my cats even know their individual names. Through conditioning, they know that when I make a specific noise, there is a result: food, petting, or play. But do they know what a name is? Who knows. The word is just a pointer.

As I dug, my list of pointing nouns, verbs, and phrases grew. A favorite is from an 85-year-old woman I met who uses an H-word: Harold. Why? A mix-up involving the Lord's Prayer. As she was teaching her granddaughter to say the prayer, the girl professed, "Our father, who art in heaven, Harold be thy name," and it stuck.

We must look beyond the word *God*—or whatever word we use—to deepen our perspective. In fact, the word doesn't even have to invoke a being, it could be *being* itself. Or a force (the Force?). It could also be the state of unitive transcendence. Of course, my wise Taoist friends remind me, "The name that can be named is not the eternal name."

The name doesn't have to stay constant either. Consider water. Constantly transforming, water can be solid, liquid, or gas. We can experience it as clouds, snow, humidity, or rain. (Recently, physicists even documented a mysterious "second state" of liquid water—it starts to act exceedingly unpredictable between 40 and 60 degrees Celsius.) Waves appear out of the ocean with "thingness," then dissolve back into the ocean from which they came. Our perspective might morph too, depending on the context.

We can each chart our own path, defining our own terms. So I'd like you to envision sacred pointing words (such as the G-word or H-word) as placeholders. A placeholder is originally a mathematic term. It's used when the exact item is not yet known—so it saves a place. At the risk of triggering a painful algebraic flashback, you might recall working with placeholders in something like this: $x = y + z$. Placeholders stand in for things you want to find out but don't have the answer to yet. By using a pointer word, you can continue your spiritual journey without having to definitively define what it is. You can get comfortable in the not-knowing state. You can understand that [x] can be defined in an unlimited number of ways, just as $x = y + z$ can be answered $x = 50 + 50$ or $x = 75 + 25$ or $x = 99 + 1$.

Which leads us to our second experiment.

SPIRITUAL EXPERIMENT #2:
DEALING WITH THE G-WORD

1. *Turn to page 217,* where you'll find a list of 200 names and descriptions I've collected for this experiment. Locate it, then flip back here to read the remaining steps.

2. *Look at the list,* letting the words sink in. Notice how the words feel to you when you look at them. Do any words seem to stand out on the page?

3. *Circle words that resonate with you* or feel like a good placeholder to work with. Some people find their word changes based on the context they are in or the experience they are having, so you may see multiple words that are meaningful.

4. *Dig in* to any words that interest you. Research them. Meditate on them.

5. *If you feel blocked* by the idea that "whatever is greater than us individual humans" can be described in

different ways yet still have an underlying sameness, try the following:

- *Make a list of all the roles you fill in your life.* (For example, mine includes writer, traveler, book addict, sponsor, sister, New Yorker, wife, and so on.)
- *Consider how one item doesn't negate another.* You can be both a blogger *and* a yoga teacher, a father *and* a son, a massage therapist *and* a volunteer firefighter.
- *Now contemplate these questions:*
  - If you can be multiple things, why can't [x] also fulfill more than one role?
  - If different people describe you in distinct roles, then couldn't different people experience and describe [x] differently?
  - Has your experience of [x] changed over time (just like your experience of relationships, jobs, and interests)?

6. *Add in any missing words* that have meaning for you below the chart.

7. *Relax.* If you don't find any words that work, you may just choose to live with the mystery represented by [x]. If so, you'll be in good company with many mystics who assert that it's impossible to define this inherently undefinable concept.

Facing our semantic issues can create a sense of relief. Understanding that we are no longer stuck with a single word or description can be liberating. Letting go of the old images that don't work for us can lead to freedom. Indeed, *letting go* may be one of the most essential spiritual endeavors out there.

Because, ultimately, your language is just a pointer for the more meaningful part: your experience of your spirituality.

Redefining spirituality

We often confuse spiritual knowledge
with spiritual attainment.
Spirituality is not a matter of knowing scriptures
and engaging in philosophical discussions.
It is a matter of heart culture, of unmeasurable strength.

MAHATMA GANDHI

* * *

As a kid, I somehow thought spirituality was limited to scripture reading, going to church, and prayer—none of which
worked very well for me. During this time, I concluded that cus-
toms from other religions or cultures weren't acceptable for me.
I struggled with wanting to follow my heart, but I was simultaneously afraid of what might happen if I did. So I did nothing.

Meanwhile, American young adults were flocking to unfamiliar religious movements, fueling families and mainstream
religious institutions to fight back with accusations of criminal
activities and brainwashing, branding new movements as cults
to be avoided. Reports about Satanic churches and this mysterious, misunderstood thing called "the occult" didn't help.
Unable to separate what was accurate criticism and what was

irresponsible scare-mongering of an otherwise valid spiritual community, I found it both perplexing and scary. Words like *heresy*, *blasphemy*, and *apostasy* came to mind, though I don't recall from who or knowing what they actually meant.

Luckily, later in life (like many of my friends), I stumbled into a yoga studio. Before long, I dove deep into Eastern philosophies and practices, such as meditation, *kirtan*, lovingkindness, *seva*, and, of course, yoga. Tiptoeing in, I sought things that felt good. That made me feel like a better person (i.e., less of an asshat). A space soon opened within me, so I tackled the S-word.

As I ambitiously poured through books, looking for the perfect definition of *spirituality*, I read many deserving of my yellow highlighter. Interspiritual innovator Wayne Teasdale, author of *The Mystic Heart*, offered: "*Spirituality* is a way of life that affects and includes every moment of existence. It is at once a contemplative attitude, a disposition to a life of depth, and the search for ultimate meaning, direction, and belonging." As the Benedictine monk Brother David Steindl-Rast suggests: "Sometimes people get the mistaken notion that spirituality is a separate department of life, the penthouse of our existence. But rightly understood, it is a vital awareness that pervades all realms of our being. Someone will say, 'I come alive when I listen to music,' or 'I come to life when I garden' ... Wherever we come alive, that is the area in which we are spiritual."

Yet I pined for a definition that was both meaningful *and* concise. So the search went on.

Visual descriptions abounded: A tree with one trunk and many different spiritual branches. A single mountain with many paths to traverse it. A river of wisdom tapped by many wells. These metaphorical definitions were indeed beautiful, but I needed something tactical, actionable. (Yes, I like to make binders, spreadsheets, and to-do lists. I'm *that* kind of nerd.)

So I created my own definition. And I'm officially challenging you to consider it while reading this book:

[Spirituality] = deeper perspective + higher purpose

In each moment of my life, this equation provides a quick way to see if I'm on track. Cultivating a deeper perspective enables me to see beyond my own needs to the interconnectedness we all share. Living with higher purpose helps me make daily choices which support that connection. And what fuels all parts of this equation is what many people refer to as *spiritual practice*.

* * *

At first, the word *practice* spurred negative childhood flashbacks for me: "Get off that computer and practice your piano, Sarah," and "Practice makes perfect!" So I looked for a new term with less baggage. Unfortunately, the often-used alternative *spiritual discipline* didn't get me much further. My thesaurus didn't offer any winners. And I swear Siri laughed at me.

The word that finally seemed to land for me was *moments*. The word *moment* is approachable; it doesn't require too much commitment. Thinking about doing something for a moment doesn't freak me out.

This book offers ideas for cultivating spiritual moments. To dissolve yourself into a bigger whole. To be able to be both yourself, and yet something greater than yourself at the same time. To be in the flow (in psychological terms) or in the zone (in sports terms). Yes, you could also say to be strong with the Force (in Jedi terms). You know you're *in a moment* when:

- You are completely absorbed in what you are doing.

- You are totally focused on the present moment, you glimpse timelessness.
- Worries slip away, as you feel a calm inner clarity.
- You may perceive your sense of reality expanding, trading your concept of the small "I" for a greater connected whole.

In these moments, spirituality and science overlap each other. Neurotheologians work in the space where neurology, spirituality, religion, and philosophy intersect. And they have plenty to say on the topic of what happens in our brains when we have spiritual experiences. Dr. Andrew Newberg is one of the leading voices on this subject. His research reveals that research subjects involved in meditation (spiritual or secular) and prayer have decreased activity in the part of the brain that constructs our sense of an independent self. In his book *How God Changes Your Brain: Breakthrough Findings from a Leading Neuroscientist*, he describes how various practices and rituals can affect different parts of the brain. And although spiritual experiences often defy comprehensive descriptions, people can verbalize the benefits they have *felt* after one, especially those that last over 12 minutes. Newberg affirms, "Activity involving meditation and intensive prayer permanently strengthens neural functioning in specific parts of the brain that are involved with lowering anxiety and depression, enhancing social awareness and empathy, and improving cognitive and intellectual functioning."

So what we *feel* in our spiritual moments is paramount—not our intellectual descriptions of our beliefs.

* * *

In the next section, you'll find instructions for a variety of activities, designed to inspire meaningful moments during the entire week—not just reserving our spiritual sides for a particular day or a specific building.

The activities are divided into days because our lives are. Taking our spirituality one day at a time helps us fully live in the present moment, with each dawn presenting opportunities for curiousness and exploration. Consider setting aside some "you time" each morning to read a section and try out the suggestions. Dedicating each day to a different spiritual focus encourages us to live the day fully—not just check a to-do box, "Yup, got my 10 minutes of meditation in today."

Each section starts with a description, followed by *How It Works* step-by-step instructions. Just below the steps are *Rebellious Variations* to explore. Choice is an essential value for most of us, so I've peppered in plenty. If something grabs you, check out the *Discover Deeply* resources to dive in further. Finally, jot down any "aha" thoughts about your experience, using the *Reflections & Ahas* pages.

This book includes three weeks' worth of creative activities, which build upon each previous week. Integrate these into your daily life or go all in and plan a spiritual staycation. Just as moments connect to make days, which combine into weeks, and then meld into months, each activity becomes part of a greater aliveness. By taking a spiritual smorgasbord approach, you can decide what to keep doing in future weeks and what gets tossed into the "*Meh, didn't work for me*" pile.

The only rule is: There are no rules. In the spirit of daring, always feel free to adapt anything. This is *your* journey. Write in the margins, rope in your friends, post your aha! moments on your social feeds. Above all, get started.

SPIRITUAL **MOMENTS**

MINDFUL MONDAYS

TALKING TUESDAYS

WONDER-FILLED WEDNESDAYS

TREKKING TUESDAYS

FEARLESS FRIDAYS

SEVA SATURDAYS

SANGHA SUNDAYS

WEEK 1:
Being

Truth is broadcasting 24/7,
but most of the time we're too busy
listening to the static of our busy lives to tune in.

VICTORIA PRICE

* * *

Be here now. Three simple words.

Immortalized by spiritual teacher Ram Dass, these words have been on society's collective lips for over 45 years. Yet for many of us, this phrase is still aspirational. With one foot in the past and one foot in the future, we're never experiencing what's going on in the present. So just what is it about merely *being* that is so difficult?

The ability to be seems hidden or forgotten, undervalued in our hurried, high-performing lives. Identifying with what we do, what we have, or what we might become, we have lost track of what we are. As the spiritual teacher A.H. Almaas, founder of the Diamond Approach to Self-Realization, muses in his book *Unfolding Now*, "How can my atoms, which are scattered, vibrating, and oscillating in some kind of frenzy, slow down, collect, and settle here as what I am?"

Being spiritual is not about changing who we are. It's about sinking more fully into what we already are. My mentor Rev. David Wallace once offered me his own three-word spiritual instruction: *Notice and inquire.* It seems to me that these three words give us a hint on how to be here now. He didn't say, "Notice, inquire, and find the perfect answer." Nope. Instead, we observe and we inquire, because, as Almas puts it, "Inquiry is based on an open and curious desire for knowing the truth of your experience exactly as it is."

So let's get curious.

Mindful Monday

Candy is nature's way
of making up for Mondays.

ANONYMOUS

* * *

Monday gets a bad rap. Often the transition from free days to work ones, Monday can feel like a slap in the face, or masquerade as an ending. But that also makes the day a beginning and an opportunity. Instead of listening to the constant static of our usual busyness, we can tap into the stillness that lies beneath it.

My perceptive friend Zulma endlessly reminds me that I am supposed to be a human *being*, not a human *doing*. And she's on to something. Every moment of my life seems filled with a task screaming for my attention, something *to do*. I suspect this idea resonates with more than a few of us. But I think we're meant to be more than a giant human version of an ant farm.

What if today all we had to do was to notice our being? To discern the eternal silence under the daily noise? Let's ease into the week with a mellow activity designed to encourage glimpses of deeper being.

WEEK 1: BREATHE

Most of the time, we breathe without thinking about it. Our bodies have the amazing ability to keep us breathing involuntarily without much effort. Ordinarily, we only spend time consciously thinking about our breaths if we have health problems (like COPD, sleep apnea, or bronchitis) or are super active (perhaps running a 5K, getting immersed in hot yoga, or summiting our favorite mountain).

But not all animals have the luxury of subconscious breath control. For example, dolphins and whales are mandatory conscious breathers. Dolphins use their mouths for capturing and eating prey, and their ingenious blowhole for breathing, typically four or five times per minute, when on the water's surface. Unlike humans, dolphins must think about inhalations and exhalations. Dolphins never fall completely asleep, and part of their brain remains alert at all times for regulation (and to keep one eye open for predators).

So what happens if we get our metaphorical dolphin on and consciously look at our breathing? A lot.

Healthwise, research shows that slow, focused breaths can lower stress and anxiety, improve coping skills, help people deal with substance abuse, improve our general sense of wellbeing, and boost our self-esteem. Spiritually, conscious breathing can help slow the mind and get us in touch with a more expansive consciousness. In fact, there's a long lineage of this spiritual practice—mainly out of the Buddhist, Taoist, and Vedic traditions—to connect us to our vital life force, also known as *Qi* (pronounced *chee*) or *prana*.

Breathwork is the gateway drug to all of our Mindful Mondays activities. The following exercise is based on a Zen counting meditation. It's pleasantly—and positively—addictive.

HOW IT WORKS

1. *Silence* your phone, computer, or anything around you that might ring, ding, or vibrate.

2. *Sit so that your back is straight,* allowing for natural movement of the breath within your body. No, you don't need to invest in a fancy meditation cushion. A chair works just fine.

3. *Make your eyes comfortable.* This practice can be done with your eyes closed, or with your gaze softly resting on a spot on the floor, a live plant, or a shimmering candle. It's important to keep your eyes resting, rather than staring sharply, looking around, or otherwise bringing distractions to your mind.

4. *Pay attention to your breath.* Notice your belly rising and falling; the movements in your chest; and the passing of thoughts as they come and go, like clouds across the sky.

5. *Count each breath silently in your mind.* At the end of the inhale, count *one*. At the end of the exhale, count *two*. Continue until you get to *five*. If you hit *six*, notice that your mind has wandered, and gently pull it back to *one*. If you find yourself wondering what is for dinner, gently pull yourself back to *one*. If you feel irritated at the noise coming from the room next to you, start again at *one*. Avoid judging the wandering. It's totally normal. Our minds are made to think, and they will think—around 50,000 thoughts a day! Just direct yourself to counting *one, two, three, four, five*.

6. *Feel your awareness sharpen.* After you've been counting for a while, you may hear sounds around you more distinctly, you may feel the temperature (or weather) more precisely. Stay with the breath.

7. *Return to your day slowly.* When you are done, avoid jumping up quickly to check your texts or social feed. Move as if your body is on half speed, easing into activity slowly and deliberately.
8. *Repeat throughout the day.* How often? Whenever you need a little peace. Breathing addictions are healthy addictions.

REBELLIOUS VARIATIONS

For math haters: Let's face it, some people have anxiety around numbers, perhaps from old math or accounting wounds. If counting is giving you anxiety, change to using the word *in* on the inhale and *out* on the exhale.

Choose your own number: Try counting to a number that is meaningful to you. For example, try your personal lucky number; 12-steppers, try counting to 12.

Count only exhales: In this variation, do not think a number when inhaling, only when exhaling. Each inhale and exhale combine into a whole breath which is counted.

Abandon counting: Eventually, you may not need numbers as a focus to keep your mind single-pointed. Abandon the numbers, and just watch the breath.

Use a phrase: A phrase, often called a *mantra**, assists the mind by providing something for it to land on. My prized combination of words (no surprise) is taken from *Star Wars: Rogue One*: "I'm one with the Force" (on inhale); "The Force is with me" (on exhale). Of course, there are innumerable traditional spiritual phrases to choose from, including: *Om Mani Padme Hum, Pura Vida, Sat-Chit-Ananda, Allahu Akbar, Baruch atta Adonai, Kyrie Eleison,* or *Om Namah Shiva.* Or stick to English and simply repeat: "I am peace."

Use some tunes: For many people, ambient music can help focus the mind on the breath. In fact, studies show that music can help activate the same parts of the brain as meditation and prayer, helping calm us, increase empathy, and release our brain's happy drug: dopamine.

The reflex: Schedule a reflexology or massage session. As the therapist's hands move up your body, focus on breathing in. As they move towards your feet, concentrate on breathing out.

Cat gazing: Hands-down, my favorite breathing meditation is with our cat Deacon. Many mornings, while I am sleeping on my back, he nestles himself on my lower legs. I become aware of his tiny, furry, black body rising and lowering. From this awareness, I tune into his breaths. With me matching my inhales and exhales to his, we become a melded being, resting in our breath. Warning: This exercise can make it difficult to get out of bed.

DISCOVER DEEPLY

- Download *The Breathing App.*
- Explore *Pranayama*** breathwork at a yoga studio near you to discover the benefits of the irritation-relieving Victorious Breath or cleansing Skull Shining Breath.
- Read *The Mantram Handbook: A Practical Guide to Choosing Your Mantram and Calming Your Mind* by Eknath Easwaran.
- Listen to the audiobook *Mantras: A Beginner's Guide to the Power of Sacred Sound* by Thomas Ashley-Farrand.
- Take a free class on using mindfulness with animals at trust-technique.com.
- Read *Guardians of Being: Spiritual Teachings from Our Dogs and Cats* by Eckhart Tolle, illustrated by Patrick McDonnell.

NOTES

* The mantra is an ancient practice, but these days, the word *mantra* sometimes is used synonymously with *motto*, so I'd like to make a distinction. A motto is a short phrase that gets to the essence of the beliefs of a person, group, or organization. It often describes a mission, vision, or goal. On the other hand, a mantra is lifted from a spiritual tradition, usually those from the East, including Hinduism and Buddhism. Although mantras are often printed on T-shirts, yoga mats, and coffee mugs, their power is in the vibration of the syllables, which are considered sacred. For example, the seed sound of many mantras, *Om*, is said to contain the energy of the entire Universe.

** Pranayama is the Sanskrit word used to describe breath work, which combines the words *prana* for *life force* and *ayama* for *extension*. The practice centers on different poses and breathing techniques, and is included in many yoga classes. If you find yourself drawn to breathing practices, consider looking into Victorious Breath, Skull Shining Breath, or Lion's Breath, just to name a few.

Talking Tuesday

Tuesday's child is full of grace.

ATTRIBUTED TO A.E. BRAY

* * *

Yeah, and Tuesday's child has always irritated me. Who exactly is this child, anyway? I was born on Wednesday. According to A.E. Bray's classic nursery rhyme, which assigns attributes to children based on their day of birth, that means I'm "full of woe." Consequently, I'm still a bit resentful of Bray's lovely grace-filled child. (And possibly Monday's fair-faced one as well.)*

But wait. It's time to get a deeper perspective, right? Probing with a quick search for "Tuesday's Child," I got a well-needed spiritual slap in the face. A nonprofit named Tuesday's Children has worked for more than a decade to provide "a lifetime of healing for those whose lives have been forever changed by terrorism and traumatic loss." Doh!

Moving past my personal resentments and the baggage I've assigned to certain words is a constant part of my spiritual journey. Sometimes my list seems insurmountable: *grace, blessing, gratitude, prayer, divine,* and even *sacred.* I'm not ready to toss these words into my sacred trash just yet, but sometimes they do linger on the can's ledge. These words seem to belong to softer, quieter people. My spirituality is often fluorescent orange with a thumping bass beat. Plenty of overtly spiritual words seem paradoxically incongruent.

On Monday, we eased in, working with an action we are used to doing naturally: breathing. Today we kick it up a notch and tackle the B-word: *blessing*. Some of you may be ready to run for the hills, screaming, "Don't go there!" Your baggage around this word may be tempting you to yell, "Screw Tuesday!" and move on. But I promise, we're going to look at this practice with our slightly-left-of-center minds, and I encourage you to stick around. See what happens.

For example, one day I professed to a friend, "I just don't get blessings," my primary reference (beyond meal times and sneezing) being, "Bless me father, for I have sinned." Somehow blessing equaled sinner. And for what reason was I supposed to ask some dude to bless me? Huh? "I hate the word *sin*," I told my friend Francine. "It's used by many people in such hurtful ways." But as I began to rant on and on about the word *sin* and its misuse, my very keen friend cut me off with, "Um, Sarah, what the hell do you think 'May the Force be with you' is?"

Curses! Foiled again!

WEEK 1: MAY THE FORCE BE WITH YOU

I realized I've had a long history of doing blessings. Odd ones, but blessings nonetheless.

Many afternoons during elementary school, my mother would yell "SARAH!" from the kitchen upon opening my school lunchbox and finding yet another dead chipmunk. It made little sense to my mother but made complete sense to me. Raised as a preacher's kid, I frequently visited funeral homes with my father. So I deduced that these animals needed burial in the bushes in our front yard. Unfortunately, at that age, I lacked the language to explain these actions convincingly, so I earned frequent lectures on germs. Unhindered, my connection with these animals remained, and I buried the animals gently with a small service ending with "May the Force be with you, chipmunk."

Of course, lurking neighbors would inform me: "Those are *just* animals. These things happen. They should learn to stay out of the road." And as I got older and questioned the ways in which I saw animals being mistreated, I was offered rationalizations such as: "God made us dominion over the animals. They are here for our use." Yikes. Folding my arms across my chest, I created a force field around myself. Increasingly feeling unconnected to those around me, I tried to hide what I felt. I became embarrassed by both burials and blessings.

Then I met the man who would become my husband. As we were driving one day, he smacked his right hand over his heart. Now, he's a bit older than I am, so I thought, "My God, he's having a heart attack. This relationship is never going to work." Nervously, I asked him, "Are you okay?" To which he replied, "I'm sending gratitude to Spirit for the life of that animal." I looked out the window, realizing excitedly, *he means that dead animal! That roadkill!* And I knew I had found my soul mate.

Of course, I promptly adopted this practice. And we became a couple of driving heart-smackers. Then on one drive, after I smacked my right hand over my heart, my husband grinned, looked at me, and said, "Um, Sarah? That was a tire." I blushed a bit in embarrassment, and then implored, "Um, Sean? Yeah,

I know. That was a blessing for the Earth, and the trash that covers her." And we both kinda giggled.

But when I look at this in hindsight, there is a profound lesson about blessing here. It affirms that our words of compassion do not have to be limited to clergy, religious institutions, or any specific tradition. Blessing does not require a particular ritual, nor does it have to occur only for a planned event. It can be done anywhere, by anyone. (*May the odds be ever in your favor!*)

In his (incredibly thorough) book *Blessing: The Art and the Practice*, American spiritual philosopher and self-described practical mystic David Spangler defines blessing as tapping into one's inner spirit to create "a good deed on steroids." Then he explains, "In practicing the art of blessing, we are really practicing being connected.... Surely a blessing is also a flow of life force between ourselves and others or between ourselves and the sacred. It's an act of connection. It restores through love a circulation of spirit among us that may have become blocked, forgotten, or overlooked. It reconnects us to the community of creation."

If you find yourself still struggling with the concept of blessing, or the word itself, try out these related ideas: being grateful, giving thanks, dedicating, saying grace, giving peace, or being kind. In many ways, the practice is about *being* rather than *doing*. You'll begin to see moments in your day in which you can offer a silent, verbal, or physical blessing, or to say words for the hope of healing our planet or for the life of that animal on the side of the road.

The practice can take myriad forms and be done in innumerable ways, which makes it hard to define the steps. Instead, I'm offering some thought-starters, followed by suggestions from some of my ingenious friends.

HOW IT WORKS

1. *Start your day by tuning in* to the flow of life force within yourself. Perhaps repeat Monday's breathing practices to get your flow going.
2. *With breakfast (even if it's just coffee), try a blessing.* Consider saying one each time you eat today. Here's an easy but powerful blessing from author, environmentalist, and animal rights activist John Robbins:

> *May all be fed.*
> *May all be healed.*
> *May all be loved.*

3. *While kicking your day into gear,* think about what you are grateful for. Create your own blessings, using the starter "May."
4. *Throughout the day, expand beyond yourself.* For each person you pass who looks like they are having a hard day, repeat silently: *May you find peace.*
5. *Continue looking for moments of blessing.* Say *Gesundheit* when someone sneezes. Offer a *May the Force be with you!* to someone.
6. *End your day with a blessing.* Recently, while staying at a New York City hotel, I noticed that my phone had a button on it to "Hear a bedtime story." I pushed the button. After a short, guided meditation played through the phone, I heard the following blessing: "No matter what happens, tomorrow will be epic if I want it to be." Wise words to head to sleep by, indeed.

REBELLIOUS VARIATIONS

Positive vibes: Shamanic Reiki practitioner Laura Klein offers, "I send this silent thought out to others, 'May the universe conspire to bring you peace and joy.'"

Presence moment: Human rights activist Barbara Becker stops at noon each day when her neighborhood's church bell rings: "I stop whatever I'm doing and go to the window for a moment of presence."

In the car: For the past three years, interfaith minister Donna Knutson has blessed all the cars that come towards her: "It's a practice that expands the surrounding area all at once so that I take in a large space visually all at one time. I started the practice because we can't 'see' who is coming towards us in metal and steel, so this was a barrier I wanted to transcend."

For those in trouble: Massage therapist Darby Mackenzie Line says a blessing each time she passes an accident or sees an ambulance speeding by with lights and siren on, silently offering, "May all beings be safe and free from pain and suffering" while sending light to whoever is involved. She asserts, "More than once I've felt 'Thank you' coming back."

Roadkill remembrances: Animal advocate and lifelong student Leann Lydon divulged, "Every time I see an animal killed in the road, I offer up a brief prayer that it died without suffering and that its spirit made it safely home."

For those grieving: Rev. Nicole Losie, chaplain for the Toledo Fire and Rescue Department, noted, "I bless all involved in every funeral procession I see. I turn off the music, interrupt any conversation I'm having, stop what I'm doing (except the driving) and silently pray for the safe return of deceased to Spirit or whatever comes next for the person, his/her loved ones, all involved in the procession, all involved in any care required while the person was still alive and after death, everyone I can think of. Then I go back to the music/audiobook/conversation, whatever. I've done this for probably 15 or so years. It just happened one time; I felt compelled, and then it became a practice."

DISCOVER DEEPLY

- Light a virtual blessing candle for a friend in need of support at gratefulness.org/light-a-candle.
- Read *Blessing: The Art and the Practice* by David Spangler.
- Read *99 Blessings: An Invitation to Life* by Brother David Steindl-Rast.
- Get involved with Blessings in a Backpack to help elementary school children across America who might otherwise go hungry. See blessingsinabackpack.org for ways to help.

NOTES

* Although for some reason I always assumed A.E. Bray was a man, A.E. stands for Anna Eliza. It's not clear if Anna Eliza, who was born in 1790, wrote the nursery rhyme or merely was the first person to record it (in *Traditions of Devonshire*). Apparently, there was a long tradition of foretelling the fate of children based on birth days. Of course, the exact future of the child differs according to which version of the rhyme you read.

Wonder-filled Wednesday

Uh-oh! Guess what day it is??
Guess what day it is! Huh, anybody?
Julie! Hey, guess what day it is??
Ah, come on, I know you can hear me.
Mike Mike Mike Mike Mike

CALEB THE CAMEL

* * *

It's hump day, of course. The middle of our modern work-week. Popularized in the 1960s, the term *hump day* gained an astonishing comeback in 2013 with insurance company Geico's Caleb the Camel ads. Wednesday has since become so synonymous with camels, it's likely to lose its original association with the Old English *Wōdnesdæg*, the day of the chief god of Norse mythology: Odin (*Wōden*). While our modern Caleb is known for his obnoxiousness, old Odin was associated with seemingly contradictory traits: wisdom, war, poetry, healing, ecstasy, and magic.

Magic is an underutilized concept in our modern scientific world, isn't it? In our quest to discover how everything works, we're skeptical of things we cannot explain or prove. We're always weaving from here to there, from this seemingly important task to that ostensibly critical task. But how often do we stop to notice brilliance in our midst, to see the wonder around us? To be amazed. To be awed. To *be*.

There is a sacred connection that underlies everything. Undeniably, the first step in getting beyond our own demanding egos is to see this connection. When we look at splendid things—the rainbow after a storm, the soaring mountains of the Himalaya, a newborn kitten—awe is instantly present. But the challenge is seeing the amazing in everything—in the meager things, the supposedly mundane, the hard times, the sad times, the painful times. As writer and philosopher G.K. Chesterton noted, "It is one thing to be amazed at a gorgon or a griffin, creatures which do not exist; but it is quite another and much higher thing to be amazed at a rhinoceros or a giraffe, creatures which do exist and look as if they don't."

We live in an age where scientific fact is often prized over mystery, where we regularly presume there is a perfectly scientific explanation for everything going on. Yet that's not the case. It's estimated that 95 percent of the Universe is composed of matter or energy that is not visible: 68 percent is dark energy and 27 percent is dark matter (neither of which is to be confused with *the dark side*; nor is *dark* a moral judgment here). NASA admits, "More is unknown than is known. We know how much dark energy there is because we know how it affects the Universe's expansion. Other than that, it is a complete mystery. But it is an important mystery."

Astrophysicist Neil deGrasse Tyson, in his wonder-filled book *Astrophysics for People in a Hurry*, agrees, "Most of the universe is made of stuff about which we are clueless." He then adds, "The universe is under no obligation to make sense to you." Indeed.

This Wōdnesdæg, let's suspend certainty in search of wonder.

WEEK 1: AMAZING EVERYTHING

Being amazed means letting go of figuring everything out. When observing something, we stay in the moment, letting the felt sense of astonishment, amazement, and wonderment seep into us. Like breathing and blessing, radical amazement can be a mode of being.

HOW IT WORKS

1. *Start your day by tuning in* to the flow of life force within yourself. Perhaps repeat Monday's breathing practices to get your flow going. Consider offering a quick blessing with your breakfast.
2. *Step outside and look up.* Observe the vastness. Breathe in and out slowly, contemplating how far "up" is. Notice the movement of any clouds and the feeling of any warmth from the Sun, which is nearly 93 million miles from you.
3. *Find a place to sit quietly.* Consider the following ideas:
   - *You are a tiny part of a massive galaxy*, one of over one hundred billion galaxies, with the nearest 600,000 light years from you.
   - *Each year,* a thousand tons of Martian rocks rain down on Earth from nearly 34 million miles away.
   - *At night,* the nearest star will be 25 trillion miles from where you are sitting.

- *Right now,* you can only see about 0.0035 percent of the light spectrum around you. The rest is invisible to the naked human eye.
- *You are one* of over seven billion humans among 8.7 million more species of life on Earth.

4. *Close your eyes gently* and consider how small you are, one tiny blip in an ever-expanding, increasingly connected universe. *Amazing.*

5. *Open your eyes.* Look at your hand, then at your foot. Consider these ideas:
   - *Around 10,000 different species of microorganisms* call you home.
   - *Your body* is made up of around 37.2 trillion cells, 2 billion of them in your heart alone.
   - *Your nose can recognize* almost a trillion different scents.
   - *Information is zooming* along your nerves at about 250 miles per hour.

6. *Close your eyes* and consider how large you are: An entire world lives within you. *Amazing.*

7. *Continuing your day, cultivate radical amazement.* Contemplate your world as you pass through it. Let *amazing* be your word of the day.

REBELLIOUS VARIATIONS

Go with the flow: Ponder these words of the Greek philosopher, Heraclitus: "You cannot step twice into the same river." Spend some time today observing water: a river, rain puddle, or even your tap. Watch how the water is in a constant state of transition, never static. Consider the implications of your own body being 45 to 60 percent water, which is replaced about every 16 days.

Grateful amazement: After any moment of awe or wonder, take time to express gratitude, perhaps tossing out a hearty "Thank you" into the universe.

Be curious, like George: Spend your day like the adorable (and inquisitive!) orphaned chimpanzee, George. When you see something that grabs your attention, probe further with questions. Author and producer Brian Grazer, in his *New York Times* bestseller, *A Curious Mind: The Secret to a Bigger Life,* proposes: "Curiosity is a state of mind. More specifically, it's the state of having an open mind. Curiosity is a kind of receptivity. And best of all, there is no trick to curiosity. You just have to ask one good question a day and listen to the answer."

Cloud gazing: If you are someone whose neck seems to be always curled down towards a screen, try reversing your position, stretching upward to check out the wonder above you, from the clouds' incredible variety of shapes, to the way they seem to float across the sky like thoughts through your mind, to the occasional auspicious rainbow. It's easy to get hooked on the sky.

Reach for the stars: Continue beyond our visible Universe, by visiting a local science museum or observatory. (Long live the retro laser light show.)

DISCOVER DEEPLY

- Read *I Asked for Wonder: A Spiritual Anthology of Abraham Joshua Heschel,* edited by Samuel H. Dresner.
- Watch the mind-blowing three-minute animation *The Inner Life of the Cell* from XVIVO Scientific Animation and Harvard University on YouTube.
- Read *A Curious Mind: The Secret to a Bigger Life* by Brian Grazer and Charles Fishman.

- Read *How to Read Water: Clues & Patterns from Puddles to the Sea* by Tristan Gooley.
- Watch *Cosmos: A Spacetime Odyssey*, Seth MacFarlane and Neil deGrasse Tyson's excellent remake of Carl Sagan's classic series.
- Read *Astrophysics for People in a Hurry* by Neil deGrasse Tyson.

Trekking Thursday

This must be Thursday.
I could never get the hang of Thursdays.
ARTHUR DENT (IN **THE HITCHHIKER'S GUIDE TO THE GALAXY**)

* * *

Yet Thursday is the day that Arthur begins the most exciting journey of his life. From his house being torn down, to Earth being vaporized, to being shot into space by a race of aliens known as the Vogons*, it happened on Thursday.

Sadly, Thursday is sometimes jokingly called "Friday Eve," or "the thing that's blocking Friday." We're going to take our cue from Arthur Dent, and make Thursday memorable by getting our trekking on. We'll explore strange new worlds, seek out new life, and boldly go where no one has gone before! As *Star Trek*'s Captain Jean-Luc Picard said, "Seize the time: Live now! Make now always the most precious time. Now will never come again."

But wait, I don't mean *that* kind of Trek. (I can see how I went there though, what with all the *Star Wars* references. It's only fair to throw in something for any smoldering Trekkies.) Unless you are reading this book after Elon Musk has addicted us to cheap space travel, we'll need to focus our trekking here on Earth. It's time to wander where Mother Nature is strong and the Wi-Fi is weak.

I can think of no better inspiration for wandering than naturalist John Muir. After his first visit to Yosemite in 1868, he returned nonstop for decades. His prolific writing filled volumes, introducing city people to the wilds of the Western United States. Eventually, Muir was pulled back to society to lobby for the Earth, cofounding the Sierra Club and becoming an unrelenting preservationist, the "Father of our National Parks."

Likely you've seen his quotes in your social media feed. His wise words abound there: "The clearest way into the Universe is through a forest wilderness," or "Of all the paths you take in life, make sure some of them are dirt," or "And into the forest I go, to lose my mind and find my soul." But the one I adore most is: "When we try to pick out anything by itself, we find it hitched to everything else in the Universe." Muir is my Yoda of the woods.

So many of our spiritual traditions speak of oneness, the unity or the Uni-verse. Sacred texts describe an absence of separation: how each thing is related to another thing related to another thing until we have no-thing but one big thing which is everything. From the Lakota's worldview of interconnectedness (*Mitákuye Oyás'iŋ*), to science's *Initial Singularity*, to the natural harmony of *Tao*, to the allness of the Vedic *Aham Brahmasmi* and the oneness of Buddhist nonseparation, we find words trying to explain a worldwide concept: *Everything is connected.* Muir's wisdom reminds us that our words are only descriptions of our experience: "I only went out for a walk, and finally concluded to stay out till sundown, for going out, I found, was really going in." His words urge us to seek that moment of complete immersion in nature when the edges of your view start to fade, and there's a sense that you are no longer just you.

WEEK 1: MAY THE FOREST BE WITH YOU

Dr. Qing Li, chairman of the Japanese Society for Forest Medicine, seeks to explain just why we feel so good when we are enveloped by nature—specifically around trees and especially in forests. Through a scientific perspective, he suggests proof for what Muir offered through prose.

Li's recommended practice is *shinrin-yoku*, Japanese for "forest bathing," or "taking in the forest through our senses." (Don't fret, all clothes will be kept on, and no soap is needed.) Consider these benefits from Li's studies: lowered stress hormones, decreased fight/flight anxiety, increased ability to rest and recover, lowered blood pressure, improved sleep, and improved mood. In his visually stunning book *Forest Bathing: How Trees Can Help You Find Health and Happiness*, Li also elaborates on forest bathing's spiritual benefits: "Immersed in the natural world, we can experience the miracle of life and connect to something larger than ourselves. Nature takes our breath away and breathes new life into us."

Today we'll seek a state of connectedness by going out to go in. Unlike Muir, most of us do not live in the shadow of Yosemite or another stunning National Park. (And I didn't give you any warning yesterday to pack for a quick trip to the forests of Japan.) So we'll start by merely finding a green spot nearby. May the forest be with us!

HOW IT WORKS

Part 1:

1.   *Start by tuning in* to the flow of life force within yourself.

2. *Soften your eyes* and recall yesterday's wonder practice. Think about the expansiveness of the Universe, and the abounding miracles going on right now in your body.
3. *Mentally scan through your schedule for today.* Where can you find 20 minutes (or more) to wander? Do you drive past a trail on your way to work? Is there a tree-filled park nearby where you could spend your lunch break? Now set a phone alarm so you don't forget to head out for your wander.

Part 2:

4. *Before starting your wander,* try this tip I picked up from Ruth Baetz in *Wild Communion: Experiencing Peace in Nature*: Leave your nagging thoughts behind. Jot down this sentence: "I'm leaving behind" and follow it with anything you are ruminating about (what you need to pick up at the store, how to pay the phone bill, your long to-do list).
5. *Silence your phone* (or better yet, leave it behind as well).
6. *Wander. Bathe your senses. Repeat.* What do you see? Smell? Hear? How does the ground feel? How does the air taste? Tune in with your senses.
7. *Notice the connections.* Leaves are parts of trees, but whole within themselves. Consider cycles in progress around you: Plants live, die, become part of the soil from which they sprouted.
8. *Reflect.* After your wander, scribble any meaningful spiritual moments. Contemplate adding more wandering throughout your week.

REBELLIOUS VARIATIONS

Enlist a friend: If you are concerned about safety in your area, take a companion. Share your "I'm leaving behind" lists with each other, then wander in silence. Afterward, reflect together to see how your experiences were similar and at the same time different.

In the city: Discover nature in the unexpected. Brick is made of organic clay and shale. Feel its texture. Imagine its transformation. Solitary trees and sidewalk weeds grow against the odds, shooting up from our urbanscapes. Take a cue from this Lakota prayer, "Let me learn the lessons hidden in every leaf and rock."

Pitching in: Take a small trash bag on your wander for any trash you see along the way. Help make the area more beautiful for whoever comes after you.

You deserve a microbreak today: Can't get out today? Schedule your wander for another day. Then spend some time looking out the window at nature. A study by the University of Melbourne found that as little as 40 seconds can help restore you from mental fatigue.

Just sit: If you are mobility-challenged, lazy, weather-bound, or forest-phobic, consider quietly sitting outside instead of wandering. According to the EPA, the average American spends 93 percent of our time indoors. Getting ourselves outside can bring tremendous mental and physical benefits. And don't forget to take your shoes off. According to Li, connecting your body to the Earth can give you a super dose of powerful healing electrons.

Be Tao: While wandering, stop for a moment and be still. Follow the guidance of Lao Tzu: "Just remain in the center watching, and then forget you are there."

Bring the outdoors in: Fill your house with healing plants. (If you share your home with any four-legged roommates, make sure to check that the plants are not toxic.)

DISCOVER DEEPLY

- Watch PBS's stunning time-lapse documentary *Nature: What Plants Talk About*.
- Read *Wilderness Essays* by John Muir.
- Find forests near you at discovertheforest.org.
- Read *Forest Bathing: How Trees Can Help You Find Health and Happiness* by Dr. Qing Li.
- Order a free Forest Therapy Starter Kit at shinrin-yoku.org.
- Read *The Hidden Life of Trees: What They Feel, How They Communicate* by Peter Wohlleben.
- Join a preservation or conservation organization.

NOTES

* Vogons should not be confused with *Star Trek*'s warp-capable Vorgons. As described in *The Hitchhiker's Guide*, "[Vogons] are one of the most unpleasant races in the Galaxy. Not actually evil, but bad-tempered, bureaucratic, officious and callous. They wouldn't even lift a finger to save their own grandmothers from the Ravenous Bugblatter Beast of Traal without orders—signed in triplicate, sent in, sent back, queried, lost, found, subjected to public inquiry, lost again, and finally buried in soft peat for three months and recycled as firelighters." So, yeah, running into them would make for a terrible Thursday.

Fearless Friday

Friday: my second-favorite F-word.

ANONYMOUS

* * *

Behind Force, of course.

I suspect none of us would count *fear* among our favorites. (It might even have shown up in our sacred trash.) Fear—and its partner anxiety—can send us into a tailspin. According to the Anxiety and Depression Association of America (ADAA), about 18 percent of us deal with anxiety at a clinical level. And the rest of us are no strangers to the fight, flight, or freeze signals coming from our amygdalas. Unable to feel safe in an inconsistent, chaotic world, we remain hypervigilant, waiting for the proverbial other shoe to drop.

In her book *First, We Make the Beast Beautiful: A New Journey Through Anxiety*, Sarah Wilson provides a spot-on description of the experience of anxiety: "The tortuous human experience of having a fretful, frenzied mind that trips along ahead of us, just beyond our grip, driving us mad and leaving us thinking we've got it all terribly wrong." Wilson goes on to suggest that our anxiety comes from disconnection from *Something Else*. (Her G-word?) "It's like we're searching for a Something Else that makes us feel...what? Like we've landed, I suppose."

Our spiritual disconnection can lead to trepidation. Feeling that we aren't safe or okay (whatever that means!), we worry we won't measure up or that we'll do something wrong. Afraid we'll lose something (or someone) that is important to us, we struggle with analysis paralysis. It's no surprise to me that many of our religious narratives contain an element of facing fear. Picture these spiritual rebels in action: Moses facing his God at Sinai, Jesus on the cross at Golgotha, Arjuna preparing for battle at Kurukshetra, Buddha facing the *maras* under the Bodhi tree, and Mohammed hearing the voice of Gabriel.

These vivid stories provide models for facing fear with courage. Likewise, our history books and current news abound with stories of courage: Chief Joseph leading his people to Canada in peaceful resistance, Martin Luther King Jr. marching for equality, Emma Gonzalez remaining silent in hope of gun legislation changes.

Stories of braveness and courage saturate every society— so much that literature professor and mythologist Joseph Campbell outlined a 17-step hero's journey he identified throughout many world mythologies. Even though you might not have read Campbell's work, you've seen the steps played out in plenty of modern movies: *Indiana Jones. Harry Potter. The Matrix. Star Wars. Star Trek. Black Panther. The Lord of the Rings.* Yes, even *Monty Python and the Holy Grail.* ("We are the knights who say, 'Ni!'")

In these stories, the words *courage* and *bravery* are often used interchangeably. Yet, if we dig, we can find a nuanced difference. Bravery is daring, bold, and admirable, often centered on an outward appearance: "My, my, isn't she brave?" Or think of *The Wizard of Oz*'s Cowardly Lion, "Put 'em up, put 'em up! Which one of you first? I'll fight you both together if you want. I'll fight you with one paw tied behind my back. I'll fight you standing on one foot. I'll fight you with my eyes closed...ohh, pullin' an axe on me, eh? Sneakin' up on me, eh?"

But without courage, the lion is all bravado. Courage is the inner spring that feeds the outward fountain of bravery, facing fear not in the absence of fear, but in spite of it. I picture my little rescue cat Deacon, his tiny little body shaking, making that first step towards us for a pat, showing strength through his perceived weakness. Author and artist Mary Anne Radmacher voices this superbly, "Courage doesn't always roar. Sometimes courage is the little voice at the end of the day that says, 'I'll try again tomorrow.'"

WEEK 1: HERE I AM

Courage is a necessary facet of our spiritual journey. Courage moves us beyond bravery to fearlessness. This doesn't mean that fear isn't present; it means we stop *fearing* fear. Rather than trying to transform any problematic moment in our lives to a saccharinely-sweet positive experience, we identify "what is." Grounded in our actual experience, we learn how to handle life on life's terms more skillfully.

Psychologist and well-loved spirituality writer Leonard Felder, Ph.D., proposes a simple practice for doing just that. Blending mindfulness techniques with a single Hebrew word (followed by its translation), he provides an approach to recenter ourselves, creating a stable foundation to face fear and anxiety during the day.

HOW IT WORKS

1. *Think* of something in your life that is stressful.
2. *Close your eyes* and visualize the situation until you start to feel the symptoms of stress (a quickened heartbeat, shorter breaths, racing thoughts, etc.).
3. *Ask* yourself this question: "Where am I?"
4. *Wait* for an honest answer from within yourself.
   - It might be a description of where you are spatially.
   - You might notice that you don't feel "here," but instead feel a nonspecific sense of anxiety, agitation, or lack of focus.
   - Your inner naysayer might respond: "What's it to you?" or "This is stupid" or "Who cares?"
5. *Feel* the answer. Connect with where you are physically, emotionally, spiritually, and energetically.
6. *Take a deep breath.* Inhale and exhale slowly.
7. *Declare Hineini*: *Here I am* (pronounced he-neh-nee).
8. *Notice* if there is any shift within you. By no longer resisting where you are, and instead gently stating that you are where you are, space may open for calmness in the eye of a mental storm.
9. *Repeat* whenever you feel unsettled during the day.

REBELLIOUS VARIATIONS

Go for a combo: Alternate saying *Hineini* with any of the breath exercises from Monday.

Go to the roots: Blogger (and Rabbi) Rachel Barenblat—aka the Velveteen Rabbi—offers an inspired interpretation of the original *Hineini* prayer. Try the first four stanzas to heighten your practice: *Here I stand / painfully aware of my flaws / quaking in my canvas shoes / and in my heart. Hineini.*

Engage the root chakra: Sit in a chair. Draw your attention to the root chakra (energy center) located at the base of your spine. Tune in to the energy there. Gently close your eyes. Staying in your body, feel the power from your root chakra extend down through the chair, the floor, and into the earth below. Picture your strength as a root that spreads through the soil, branching off, creating its own robust root system entwined with the Earth. Feel this groundedness. Breathe your eyes open, remaining energetically connected to Mother Earth. From this place, say silently: *Hineini. Here I am.*

DISCOVER DEEPLY

- Read *Here I Am: Using Jewish Spiritual Wisdom to Become More Present, Centered, and Available for Life* by Leonard Felder, Ph.D.
- Watch *Finding Joe* to learn more about Joseph Campbell, the hero's journey, and archetypes.
- Read Sarah Wilson's *First, We Make the Beast Beautiful: A New Journey Through Anxiety* to learn creative exercises for curbing fear.
- Check out Parker Palmer's Center for Courage & Renewal at couragerenewal.org.
- Read Gregory Maguire's stunning modern retelling of the Cowardly Lion story, *A Lion Among Men.*

NOTES

* *Hineini* combines two Hebrew words: *hineh,* meaning *here* and *ani,* meaning *I.* Appearing just a few times in the Hebrew scriptures, the word is used as an answer to a call to higher purpose. The word is used sparingly, in big moments, where fear may be present. Hineini is not relegated to moments such as *Here I am in the DMV line.* Instead, its tone is emphatic, solid, and firm, connecting us to the bigger picture of life. In a world where we are so often coming, going, or trying to be five places at the same time, it can be powerful to take a moment to make this bold statement.

Seva Saturday

You just brought yourself another Saturday.
VICE PRINCIPAL "DICK" VERNON (IN **THE BREAKFAST CLUB**)

You just brought yourself another Saturday.
VICE PRINCIPAL "DICK" VERNON (IN **THE BREAKFAST CLUB**)

* * *

As a teen of the 1980s, I have distinct movie quotes forever embedded in my mind. Darth Vader's infamous "I am your father." Creepy Carol Anne whining, "They're hee-eere!" in *Poltergeist.* Mr. Miyagi's wise "Wax on, wax off" in *The Karate Kid.* And pretty much every line from *The Breakfast Club*, including the essential cry: "If he gets up, we'll all get up. It'll be anarchy!"

As a reckless teenager, I lusted after *The Breakfast Club*'s insolent John Bender (played by Judd Nelson) in his grungy red flannel, ripped jeans, and heavy combat boots (even though I still firmly believe the foot bandana was a misstep by the wardrobe department). Bender's crazed bravado helped hide his insecurity and pain just under the surface, which was something I identified with. As Bender went head-to-head with grumpy vice principal "Dick" Vernon in the "Eat My Shorts" tirade, my heart raced while he racked up an endless number of Saturday detentions because of his contemptuous backtalking.

Rewatching the scene recently (with my so-called enlightened adult mind), I noticed a nugget of wisdom in Vernon's speech: "You know something, Bender? You oughta spend a little more time trying to do something with yourself, and a little less time trying to impress people. You might be better off." These cringe-worthy words from my teens now spoke volumes.

Many spiritual teachings echo Vernon's sentiment: We should aspire to do something worthwhile with our lives. Some version of the Golden Rule ("Treat others like you want to be treated") appears in most religions and philosophies. Many go a step further with calls for some measure of selflessness in our actions, such as the practice of giving, charity, volunteering, or *seva*.

A Sanskrit term found in many Eastern spiritualities, seva is about selfless service: something is done without any thought of payment, reward, recognition, or even a thank you. Ram Dass (of *Be Here Now** fame) brought the word into the U.S. mainstream in the 1970s and even named the foundation he cofounded Seva Foundation. Since 1978, the foundation has helped over 3 million people regain sight through free and low-cost surgeries/eye care services.

Modern self-described yogi provocateur Daniel Scott confirms that service continues with the next generation of modern yogis and yoginis: "Seva is the karmic life preserver that keeps your spiritual head above water by helping others to stay afloat." I found Daniel where many of today's up-and-coming spiritual teachers can be found—in a blog. I noticed him, and was curious, so I inquired.

As I asked Daniel questions, I quickly learned that he indeed qualifies as a spiritual rebel. Rather than seeing himself as a yoga teacher accumulating followers with blind faith in *him*, Daniel seeks to help others find faith in themselves: "I believe in the power of the connections that we create, not just to other people, or other ideas or causes, but also within ourselves. How we connect with our self is how we connect with the world."

For many of us, as we connect with the world, seva is not just one-sided. The world is round, and our actions are, in essence, round as well. True, we help others, but we're also helping ourselves, in a fully circular connection. Like Daniel's life-preserver image, which I probed him to expand on. "When I feel lost, or sad, or challenged, or just not in my highest capacity, I oftentimes find that it's almost easier to help others because it gives me a sense of feeling like I have something to give and have worth," he explained. "Even if it's just buying a cup of coffee for someone or just listening. We always think that giving has to be something that's material based, but sometimes just giving presence, just holding space, or filling space with quiet support is more than enough to help some other people work through some really crazy shit."

Daniel reminds us that service doesn't have to be big, Instagram-worthy actions. It's a state rather than a specific activity. Another of my wise sages, One Spirit founder Diane Berke, confirms the importance of service in her book, *The Gentle Smile: Practicing Oneness in Daily Life* (originally published in 1995): "We live in this world with other people, and the 'dailiness' of our lives is very much made up of encounter and relationship—from the casual, passing, seemingly chance encounters with strangers on the subway, in the check-out line at the grocery store, or riding in the elevator, to the interactions of our work and social relationships, friendships, love and family relationships. Service cannot be separated from relationship and, in a very real sense, relationship cannot be separated from service."

Melding the related concepts of kindness, caring, charity, volunteering, giving, and paying it forward, we find a robust way of being. Today, we'll look at service through this lens.

WEEK 1: 7.7 BILLION SERVED

Luckily, many of our actions this week primed us:

- Monday, we experienced our breath.
- Tuesday, we embodied a state of blessing.
- Wednesday, we speculated on the immense and the tiny.
- Thursday, we reflected on our connections.
- Friday, we envisioned how to stand in courage.

Now, as we roll into the weekend, it's time to expand beyond ourselves—to spread our spirituality outward to some of the other 7.7 billion people on this planet. To become a karmic life-preserver, starting with our way of being, continuing through our thoughts, and flowing out into the world through our actions.

A powerful way to get started is through the practice of *Metta*, usually translated as lovingkindness.** By focusing our thoughts on the wellness of ourselves and others, we cultivate compassion, kickstarting our actions in the same direction.

HOW IT WORKS

1. *Silence* your phone, computer, or anything around you that might ring, ding, or vibrate.
2. *Start by tuning in* to the flow of life force within yourself. Perhaps repeat Monday's breathing practices to get your flow going.

3. *Place your hands on your chest softly.* Feel the beating of your heart.
4. *Take a deep breath.* Feel the expansion and the contraction of your lungs.
5. *Say each line* below out loud slowly:

> May I be free from fear.
> May I be returned to wholeness.
> May I be filled with loving kindness.
> May I be of service to others.
> May I be happy, peaceful, and at ease.

6. *Place your hands in your lap softly, with your palms facing upwards.* Feel the energy emanating from your hands.
7. *Take a deep breath.* Feel the flow of air within you.
8. *Envision someone you love.* Picture the person in your mind, their hands connecting to yours.
9. *Say each line* below out loud slowly:

> May you be free from fear.
> May you be returned to wholeness.
> May you be filled with loving kindness.
> May you be of service to others.
> May you be happy, peaceful, and at ease.

10. *Take a deep breath.* Feel the inhalation and exhalation.
11. *Envision someone with whom you are having difficulty.* Picture the person in your mind.
12. *Say each line* below out loud slowly:

> May you be free from fear.
> May you be returned to wholeness.
> May you be filled with loving kindness.

May you be of service to others.
May you be happy, peaceful, and at ease.

13. *Take a deep breath. Ahhhhhh.*
14. *Envision all beings.* Imagine a long line of people stretched around the world like a giant "I'd Like to Buy the World a Coke" ad. Everyone is included. Among the "two-leggeds" pass Earth's other creatures: including the four-leggeds, the six-leggeds, and the multi-leggeds, as well as the slithering, the finned, and the winged.
15. *Grasp your hands together* to complete this giant circle of life.
16. *Say each line below out loud slowly:*

May all beings be free from fear.
May all beings be returned to wholeness.
May all beings be filled with loving kindness.
May all beings be of service to others.
May all beings be happy, peaceful, and at ease.

17. *Sit silently* for a while, noticing how these statements feel.
18. *During the day* embody these words, looking for opportunities to be of service to the people around you, acting in a state of generosity without any thought of payment, reward, recognition, or thank you.

REBELLIOUS VARIATIONS

Classic Metta: Try this classic Buddhist four-phase version: "May I be free from danger. May I have mental happiness. May I have physical happiness. May I have ease of wellbeing." Then extend it out past yourself.

Daily affirmation: Joran Slane Oppelt, owner of the Metta Center of St. Petersburg and author of *Integral Church: A Handbook for New Spiritual Communities* offers this "Affirmation of the Eight Rooms" (from his forthcoming book, *The Eight Rooms: A Key to the Universal Values We Can't Live Without*):

> I am in love and I am unattached.
> I am empty and I am changing.
> I am present and I am productive.
> I am joyful and I belong.

Extend this affirmation into lovingkindness by repeating the words first as is, then by replacing *I am* with *May you be*.

Personal psalms: Lovingkindness shows up in many spiritual traditions. In Judaism, it's referred to as *Chesed*. In fact, the book of Psalms (sacred songs) proclaims the world is built on kindness and love between people: *Olam Chesed Yibaneh*. Try my modern psalm based on the ancient priestly blessing, first for yourself, then repeating for others.

> May I/you be blessed and guarded against suffering.
> May the eternal light of the Cosmos shine upon me/you.
> May peace be with me/you.

Bring on the light: Try these invocative words based on the Hadith of Islamic tradition:

> Let there be light before me, and light behind me, and on my right light, and on my left light, and above me light, and beneath me light. May I be light.
> Let there be light before you, and light behind you, and on your right light, and on your left light, and above you light, and beneath you light. Make you be light.

The write stuff: Write your own compassion meditation. The prayer below is based on one widely attributed to St Francis (though it's unlikely he wrote it). Since the words are frequently edited and adapted, I took the liberty of tweaking them. Here's my version:

> Make me an instrument of peace.
> That where there is hatred, I may bring love.
> That where there is wrong, I may bring the spirit of forgiveness.
> That where there is discord, I may bring harmony.
> That where there is error, I may bring truth.
> That where there is doubt, I may bring faith.
> That where there is despair, I may bring hope.
> That where there are shadows, I may bring light.
> That where there is sadness, I may bring joy.
> That I may seek rather to comfort, than to be comforted.
> To understand, than to be understood.
> To love, than to be loved.
> For it is by self-forgetting that one finds.
> It is by forgiving that one is forgiven.

DISCOVER DEEPLY

- Read *The Sacred Art of Lovingkindness: Preparing to Practice* by Rabbi Rami Shapiro.
- Watch "Cultivating Loving Awareness with Ram Dass, Krishna Das, Sharon Salzberg, and Mirabai Bush" on YouTube.
- Read *The Book of Forgiving: The Fourfold Path for Healing Ourselves and Our World* by Desmond Tutu and Mpho Tutu.

- Read *Tattoos on the Heart: The Power of Boundless Compassion* by Greg Boyle.

NOTES

* Ram Dass (born Richard Alpert) developed *Be Here Now* shortly after returning from his 1970s pilgrimage to India, where he studied under guru Neem Karoli Baba (also referred to as Maharaj-ji). Originally titled *From Bindu to Ojas*, the bestselling book started as a collection of stories, spiritual techniques, and illustrations put together by Ram Dass and members of his spiritual community. Selling over two million copies, *Be Here Now* has inspired hippies and hipsters alike for over 40 years.

** The word *metta* comes to us from the Pali language from classical India. Bridging two root meanings—gentle and friend—the practice is a staple of Buddhist meditation. Although the exact phrases may differ, the essential action of Metta is a tender, heart-centered outpouring of deep wishing for ourselves, those we love, those for whom we have neutral feelings, and those that we are in conflict with.

Sangha Sunday

The next Buddha may be a Sangha.

THICH NHAT HANH

✴ ✴ ✴

For many years I had problems finding my *tribe*. Holding on tightly to my individuality, I found it hard to feel that I fit perfectly into any single group. Suffering from insecurity, I rejected some with merely a second glance. I flip-flopped between wanting to belong and wishing to be alone so I could be my authentic self.

So when I first read *Harry Potter and the Sorcerer's Stone*, I desperately wished I could try on the worn, cone-shaped Sorting Hat. (*Nitwit! Blubber! Oddment! Tweak!*) In the book, the enchanted hat magically reads each student's mind to deduce the optimal house group based on character traits. The lucky students, now sorted, would then find their forever friends and live happily ever after (at least in my mind). When I consulted the *Pottermore* website's "Discover your Hogwarts House" quiz, the virtual Sorting Hat declared me Gryffindor. However, I rebelliously proclaimed I was assuredly Ravenclaw.*

Amusingly, the quiz's results seemed to mirror my life experience, with all groups falling short of my expectations—too much *this* or not enough *that*. To cope with this tension, I'd slip on headphones, escaping to an inner private world, simultaneously disconnecting from the people around me, convinced that if I couldn't *hear* you, you couldn't *see* me. Tired of putting time into relationships that felt phony and shallow, I decided to bury my nose in a book instead, or sit home and binge-watch Netflix. Predictably, self-isolation quickly led to loneliness. Meanwhile, everyone online seemed to be having a perfect life, further fueling my desire *not* to connect.

Time alone can be rejuvenating or refreshing, but too much isolation can be clinically bad for our health. According to the American Psychological Association, loneliness and social isolation may "represent a greater public health hazard than obesity. Being connected to others socially is widely considered a fundamental human need—crucial to both wellbeing and survival." Emma Seppälä, science director of the Center for Compassion and Altruism Research and Education at Stanford University School of Medicine (wow, now that's a title) concurs. In her book, *The Happiness Track*, she notes that one in four Americans say they have no one to talk to about a personal problem. "Loneliness and lack of social connection has been linked to anxiety, depression, slower recovery from disease. It's been linked to premature death, and it's linked to suicide."

Personal contact helps us stay healthy and emotionally balanced. Two overlooked—but incredibly important—parts of feeling connected are our eyes and smiles. Research indicates that eye contact is a critical part of conversations, helping synchronize activity in certain parts of our brains to each other. What's more, we're likely to better remember people that we have eye contact with.

Similarly, when isolating, we miss the power packed into our smiles. Studies have noted that smiling can relieve stress, increase empathy, and improve relationships. It can enhance not only your mood but also the moods of those around you. When we see someone smile, mirror neurons for smiling are activated in our own neural networks, and we experience the feeling of a smile ourselves.

When we are all walking around plugged in—connected but not connected—not hearing except from our headphones, not seeing because our eyes are on our screens, we miss these opportunities to relate through our eyes and our smiles. We are losing the ability to tap into our transcendent connectedness. Spiritual author Eknath Easwaran, in his book *Words to Live By*, describes what can happen when we do connect: "When you discover that everyone is contained in you and you are contained in everyone, you have realized the unity of life, which is the divine ground of existence. Then, you are not just a person; you have become a beneficial force. Wherever you go, wherever you live, those around you will benefit from your life."

This kind of connectedness may sound unfamiliar to our ears. Ever since the founding of this country, our revolutionary culture has focused on the rights of the individual. Individuality has dominated over community, as we each relentlessly pursue the so-called American Dream. We've sorted ourselves into groups, not with a magical Sorting Hat, but instead, based on our politics, religious beliefs, and ideologies, operating in a binary world of opposites. Yet some voices encourage us to believe that peace still has a chance.

WEEK 1: GIVE PEACE A CHANCE

Vietnamese Buddhist monk and peace activist Thich Nhat Hanh (aka Thay) is a superhero in the world of peace advocacy. Spreading the message of peace and brotherhood since the 1960s, he was a formidable force in lobbying Western leaders to end the Vietnam War, and led the Buddhist delegation to the Paris Peace Talks in 1969. With over 100 books, an extensive speaking schedule, and community seeding, he's spread mindfulness, meditation, and Engaged Buddhism throughout the Western world.

It's through his work that many spiritual seekers are introduced to the concept of *sangha*. Originally the word for a Buddhist community, sangha is now often used as a generic term. In an article for *Tricycle* magazine, titled "The Fertile Soil of Sangha," Thay suggests why the sangha is vital for individuals: "With the support of friends in the practice, peace has a chance.... Your sangha—family, friends, and copractitioners— is the soil, and you are the seed. No matter how vigorous the seed is, if the soil does not provide nourishment, your seed will die. A good sangha is crucial for the practice. Please find a good sangha or help create one."

Today let's try connecting to the greater human sangha.

HOW IT WORKS

1. *Silence* your phone, computer, or anything around you that might ring, ding, or vibrate.
2. *Breathe* gently to get focused.
3. *Repeat these words* from Thich Nhat Hanh's Smiling Meditation with your breaths:
   - Breathing in, I calm my body.
   - Breathing out, I smile.

4. *Throughout the day,* reach out with your eyes. Start with people you know. Connect through your eyes before using any words, even "Hi." See what happens when you smile before you start speaking. Take time to truly see the people around you.
5. *Extend to strangers.* As you pass people you don't know, make eye contact. Then flash them a quick smile. Consider everyone as part of one human sangha. (Exercise basic safety, of course.)
6. *Notice* the reactions of people and how you feel.
7. *Scribble* your reflections.

REBELLIOUS VARIATIONS

Namast'ay connected: *Namaste* is a Sanskrit greeting in India, Nepal, and yoga/meditation centers worldwide. When used in a spiritual sense, it's commonly translated as "I bow to the divine in you." It is an acknowledgment that the light in me greets the light in you, that we have divine sameness and connection. Try silently saying "Namaste" as you meet the gaze of others.

Mirror, mirror, on the wall: Gaze into a mirror, meeting your reflection. Take a few full breaths. Silently urge your mind to let go of any expectations about the practice. Continue to breathe slowly, observing what passes through your mind. Notice how the other parts of your body feel as you connect visually to yourself. Continue for at least five minutes or longer, like until you get kicked out of the bathroom by your urgent-minded roommate or family member.

Become a soul gazer: Find a close friend who is willing to try something potentially awkward with you. Yeah, *that* friend. Set your phone timer for 10 minutes. Sit facing each other with your knees just barely touching. Gaze lightly into each other's eyes, inhaling and exhaling through your nose. Try to keep your eyes on your partner, breathing through any awkwardness. Remember, it's an experiment. See what happens. You might expand your capacity for intimacy or burst out into joyous laughter (and perhaps do both simultaneously).

Puppy-dog eyes: When your dog is calm and blissed-out, try gazing into its eyes. Takefumi Kikusui (an animal behaviorist at Azabu University in Japan) examined the impact of eye contact in dogs and their human companions. He found that with sustained gazing, oxytocin levels increased in both the dog and the human. "Oxytocin is a hormone associated with trust and maternal bonding. It increases when you're close to someone you love and gives you that warm fuzzy feeling." Ah, puppy love, indeed. (Cat lovers, stick to stroking your cat. Some cats can find staring a challenge. But stroking at an optimal rate of 40 strokes per minute may increase both your and Fluffy's oxytocin as well.)

Run, forest, run: Hands down, my favorite animal to gaze at is a forest squirrel. Squirrels are remarkably attuned to human actions, so it's best to stand still and gaze at the squirrel just past its body. Often, it will take the same pose, silently starring back. Notice how it feels to connect in stillness with a different species.

DISCOVER DEEPLY

- Watch *Human* by Yann Arthus-Bertrand.
- Try a Laughter Yoga class to experience gazing and smiling on metaphorical steroids (laughteryoga.org).
- Read *Good Citizens: Creating Enlightened Society* by Thich Nhat Hanh.
- Read *Mirroring People: The Science of Empathy and How We Connect with Others* by Marco Iacoboni.

NOTES

* According to the *Pottermore* quiz: "Gryffindor is the house which most values the virtues of courage, bravery, and determination ... Hufflepuffs value hard work, patience, loyalty, and fair play ... Ravenclaws prize wit, learning, and wisdom ... Slytherin produces more than its share of Dark wizards, but also turns out leaders who are proud, ambitious, and cunning."

WEEK 2:
Deepening

If we attempt to act and do things
for others and for the world
without deepening our own self-understanding,
our freedom, integrity, and capacity to love,
we will not have anything to give others.

THOMAS MERTON

* * *

As a book addict, my go-to path is books whenever I'm looking to expand my knowledge. Sometimes I head for a sacred
text like the Bhagavad Gita, the Dhammapada, or the Gospel of
Thomas. Other times, I reexamine a quintessential childhood
canon: *The Chronicles of Narnia, The Hobbit,* or *A Wrinkle in
Time.* I'm as likely to find wisdom from Aslan or Gandalf as I am
from the Buddha, Krishna, or Jesus. And, when it comes to the
topic of deepening, I can think of no better character to consider than Sporos, who I met in the pages of Madeleine L'Engle's
follow-up to *A Wrinkle in Time,* titled *A Wind in the Door.* In
the story, young Meg Murry sets out to overcome cosmic evil
(the Echthroi) and save her brother Charles Wallace from his

illness. Remember last Wednesday, when we considered our bodies as entire worlds, with 10,000 different species of microorganisms calling each of us home? Well, that's what's happening in *A Wind in the Door*. Little Charles Wallace's inner mitochondria are ailing, and the whole universe inside his body is at risk. Enter Sporos, a farandola located in the mitochondria of one of Charles' cells.

For Charles Wallace to live, his farandolae must "deepen." They must push through their fright of the unknown with courage to become part of a greater purpose than each one's individuality. When doing so, though, each loses the ability to move and dance on its own.

In his starring scene, Sporos must fight the urge to remain in his own self-absorbed role and consider the needs of the interconnected galactic world he lives in. An ally pleads, "You are created matter, Sporos. You are part of the great plan, an indispensable part. You are needed, Sporos; you have your own unique share in the freedom of creation."

Sporos must *deepen*.

Through this tiny character, L'Engle seeks to teach us that both the microcosm and macrocosm are part of the interdependence of everything in the Cosmos. That the small matters as much as the large. That our actions matter, because they affect others—even the others we can't see.

Amusingly, L'Engle loves sprinkling Hebrew and Greek words into her books. Profound buried meanings lie under the fantastical names of places and characters. *Sporos* is one of those words; in Greek (σπόρος), it means a seed. So let's approach Week 2 with a cosmic gardener's mind, planting seeds to nurture our understanding of the connectedness of life.

Like Sporos, we need to deepen.

Mindful Monday

* * *

WEEK 2: WITH A REBEL YAWN

If you're anything like me, somewhere during the day, you might yawn—especially on a Monday after a big weekend. But what exactly is yawning? And how can it help us in our search for spiritual moments? Let's ease into Week 2 with a quick exploration.

Yawning is still a bit of a puzzle. Theories abound on why we do it, from being tired or bored to lack of oxygen or to lower the temperature of the brain. Sometimes it signals a change in physiological states—from sleep to waking, boredom to alertness, waking to sleep, and so on. Instagram informed me a yawn was a silent scream for coffee.

Like conscious breathing, yawning can produce health benefits. Neuroscientists Dr. Andrew Newberg and Mark Waldman assert: "Yawning will physiologically relax you in less than a minute." Here are "12 Essential Reasons to Yawn Each Day," developed for their book, *How God Changes Your Brain: Breakthrough Findings from a Leading Neuroscientist*:

1. Stimulates alertness and concentration
2. Optimizes brain activity and metabolism
3. Improves cognitive function
4. Increases memory recall
5. Enhances consciousness and introspection
6. Lowers stress
7. Relaxes every part of your body
8. Improves voluntary muscle control
9. Enhances athletic skills
10. Fine-tunes your sense of time
11. Increases empathy and social awareness
12. Enhances pleasure and sensuality

Wow, and I was always taught not to yawn because it's rude. (That's because, historically, we've associated the action with boredom. Also, because we're not so fond of looking inside people's open mouths. Note to self: Always cover mouth when yawning.)

Even our pets benefit from yawning. Have you ever noticed your dog doing it after a particularly tough day or a visit to the V-E-T? Dogs often use a yawn to release stress, deal with nervousness, or get rid of pent-up energy. Similarly, my cat Buba-ji* does it after any exceptionally detailed self-grooming session. His tension released, he then drops into sound sleep.

Moving on to spiritual territory, recent neuroscience research presents some intriguing findings as well. It suggests that yawning creates a unique type of neural activity in the area of the human brain that plays a fundamental role in consciousness and self-reflection. What's more, this activity is linked to generating social awareness and creating feelings of empathy. Try yawning in a crowded room. People who "yawn back" likely have a high level of empathy—or are silently screaming at you for coffee.

Let's give it a try.

HOW IT WORKS

1. *Find a private space.* (This exercise could be a bit embarrassing in public unless you have strong self-confidence!)
2. *Silence* your phone, computer, or anything around you that might ring, ding, or vibrate.
3. *Stand up.* Stretch your arms straight up as high as you can, stretching the fingers wide, then release your arms down to your sides with an exhale.
4. *Take a deep breath*—a really full breath, stretching your mouth open like a yawn—and then exhale, sighing loudly.
5. *Pause.* Don't skip this step. Passing out is not the goal of this exercise.
6. *Repeat fake yawn-y breath.* Alternate breaths 12 to 15 more times with a short pause in between. (Most likely, your fake yawns will turn into bona fide ones.)
7. *Sink into 10 minutes* of stillness, watching your breath—or using any of last week's breathing variations that you liked.
8. *Check out the variations below* to infuse yawning into your day.

REBELLIOUS VARIATIONS

At work: Yawn when you find yourself in conflict with another person (covering your mouth, of course, and stepping into a private space first if the person is über-politically correct). Like your dog, you may find a release of the negative energy.

Constantly bombarded? Change your desktop pic to someone yawning—seeing a pic (or even reading the word *yawn*) can trigger a releasing yawn.

When you're pissed off: Nothing zaps spiritual energy like anger. Yawning is safer and way more cost-effective than tossing plates into a wall.

Before meditating: Use a yawn to kick-start your breathing or meditation session. If you're in a group, consider sharing your tips (to help others and avoid any pesky judgment).

DISCOVER DEEPLY

- Read *How Enlightenment Changes Your Brain: The New Science of Transformation* by Dr. Andrew Newberg and Mark Robert Waldman.
- See spiritual practice brain scans and learn more about neurotheology at andrewnewberg.com.
- Read *The Bonobo and the Atheist* by Frans de Waal for more on yawn contagion and empathy.
- Read *Meditations for Interspiritual Practice: A Collection of Practices from the World's Spiritual Traditions* edited by Netanel Miles-Yépez.

NOTES

* *-ji* is a suffix tacked onto the end of words as a sign of respect or reverence. Found in many of the languages of South East Asia, it can be added to names (such as Gandhi to Gandhiji) as well as objects of respect. For example, the river Ganges is often called Gangaji.

Talking Tuesday

WEEK 2: THE MIND IS LIKE TOFU. BE CAREFUL WHAT YOU MARINATE IT IN.

In my most desperate years, I acted as Mad Random DJ a couple nights each week. Not a talented DJ at a hot club. No, this was a private thing in a tiny New York City studio apartment, much to the dismay of my neighbors. Lacking coping skills for dealing with anger, I relied on cheap Merlot and a 400-disc CD player to soothe my discomfort. Unfortunately, I had never labeled even one of the CDs in the player, so I had no idea which disc was in which slot. Nights would devolve into me dumping the player upside down, freeing the CDs into a mess on the floor, and rummaging through to find the desired disc. Once I'd found it, I'd feed it back into the player and commence singing loudly whatever maudlin lyrics fit the resentment festering inside me. (*Jagged Little Pill* flashback, anyone?)

The innovative and delightfully humorous Rabbi Zalman Schachter-Shalomi taught, "The mind is like tofu. By itself, it has no taste. Everything depends on the flavor of the marinade it steeps in." Likewise, Thich Nhat Hanh recommends that we be mindful about everything we consume, including what we watch and listen to, only consuming what "can water the seed of understanding, compassion, joy, and happiness in us."

When I played Mad Random DJ, I fed angst with musical anger, sadness with tearful melodies. I dug an emotional rut. Of course, the iPod made this chaotic night ritual obsolete. And soon the cheap Merlot was a thing of the past, as I learned how to manage life without relying on wine as a miraculous elixir. Yet through the years I've missed those loud, passionate, lyrical nights and the emotional release they provided.

That is, until I found *kirtan** (pronounced KEER-tahn). Evolving from the Vedic traditions, kirtan is a call-and-response type of chanting. Usually done in groups, the performers and audience co-create a spiritual space, establishing wholeness from individual, disparate voices. Tactically, it means you sit on the floor and repeat each line the leader sings, as the musicians provide the melodious base. Yet it's nothing like kindergarten music class.

First, you'll likely be singing in Sanskrit (since the practice originated in India over 2,500 years ago). Second, no one will laugh at you for getting the lyrics (or tone) wrong. Sometimes the words are provided on paper or appear on a screen. More likely, you'll follow along by ear. But don't worry, you don't need to know Sanskrit. Just repeat what you hear. The vibration of the sound is more important than the meaning of the words. (If you develop a kirtan practice, the understanding will come—a core set of mantras, phrases, names, and words are often repeated.) You can even try just humming along to each tone. The rhythmic vibration of the sounds can calm your mind, help reduce stress, and provide more balance to your nervous system.

Author Anodea Judith has a good deal to say on the power of sound on our bodies, in her amazingly thorough book *Eastern Body, Western Mind*: "We experience resonating wave forms in many ways. When we listen to a chorus of voices or a troupe of drummers, we are immersed in a field of resonance that vibrates every cell in our body. Such a field influences the subtler vibration of consciousness and we feel pleasure, expansiveness, and rhythmic connection with the pulse of life itself." Have you ever chanted "Om" at the end of a yoga class? Kirtan is like that sound immersion—multiplied.

Here in the U.S., most conversations about kirtan eventually contain the name Krishna Das, the "Rockstar of Yoga," so dubbed when nominated for a 2013 Grammy Award. This nickname is well deserved. Krishna Das's life-changing 1970s journey to India led directly to the popularization of the chant style in the States.** In his memoir, *Chants of a Lifetime: Searching for a Heart of Gold*, Krishna Das notes that one of the goals of kirtan is to experience the Oneness, the pure awareness, that connects all of us: "We can't think our way out of feeling desperate, but when we do a practice, the walls we've constructed around our hearts begin to get broken down. We become more ourselves, not less. What do we lose except fear and unhappiness? Everything that has held us back or limited us begins to disappear from our lives. We become peace."

HOW IT WORKS

1. *Determine your optimal listening set-up.* This is about sound—so you'll need speakers or headphones connected to a device that can connect to the internet.

2. *Find a space* where you can make noise without offending anyone. (Full house? A parked car makes an excellent listening chamber.)
3. *Go to spiritual-rebel.com/kirtan, and select a piece of music* from the links list.
4. *Get your chant on.* The tracks include a chorus of imaginary friends who will help you along. Close your eyes. Meld into the sound. Sing along as you feel comfortable. The longer you chant, the more likely you are to enter into the vibrations.
5. *Notice and reflect.* After the song is finished, sit for a bit in silence. Notice how your body feels. Notice what's going on in your mind. Use the *Reflections & Ahas* pages in the back of the book to jot any profound thoughts.

REBELLIOUS VARIATIONS

Noise check: Take a quick inventory of what you audibly digest on a typical day. What is helpful? What inadvertently might be adding stress, anger, or diverting your focus?

Full-body Oms: Sit in a comfortable position. Picture the cosmos at its inception, before everything we know today existed. Now, chant the three syllables represented by the mysterious OM (pronounced A-U-M) slowly, letting each syllable transform into the next:

- AAAA – Feel this in your abdomen.
- UUUU – Notice the vibration of your voice move up to your chest.
- MMMM – Let the sound pulse in your throat and on your lips.
- Repeat three (or more) times.

Mary had a little Kriya: Clinical research on a specific exercise called Kirtan Kriya suggests that practicing it for just 12 minutes a day can improve cognition, ease depression, and activate parts of the brain that are essential for memory. Softly chant "Saa, Taa, Naa, Maa" (which represents your highest self or true identity) using the first four tones from the "Mary Had a Little Lamb" song. With each note, touch each thumb to a subsequent fingertip. (For Saa, touch your thumb to your index fingertip. Then for Taa, your middle finger, and so on.) Repeat for:

- First two minutes: Sing normally.
- Minutes 3-4: Sing in a whisper.
- Minutes 5-8: Say the syllables silently in your mind.
- Minutes 9-10: Sing in a whisper.
- Minutes 11-12: Sing normally.

Take a deep inhale, stretch your hands above your head, and then sweep them down and out slowly as you exhale.

DISCOVER DEEPLY

- Download the Insight Timer meditation app for access to kirtan on your phone. At the *Explore* screen, enter *kirtan* in the search field.
- Read *Chants of a Lifetime: Searching for a Heart of Gold* (with CD) by Krishna Das, or check out his Chai'n'Chat podcasts at krishnadas.com.
- Read *Eastern Body, Western Mind: Psychology and the Chakra System as a Path to the Self* by Anodea Judith.
- Learn to play kirtan songs on harmonium or guitar at bhaktibreakfastclub.com.

NOTES

* *Kirtan* derives from the Sanskrit word for *praise*. However, kirtan differs from standard hymns. Rather than telling a story or moral lesson, kirtan is about sinking into a praiseful feeling.

** Devotional chanting has been embedded in Indian spiritualities since the proverbial "Primordial Om" of creation (or at least for the last few thousand years). Kirtan in the U.S. owes its original roots to Paramahansa Yogananda, who led 3,000 people in chant at Carnegie Hall in New York City in 1923 as part of the first migration of Eastern thought to the West. More than 40 years later, the Beatles' George Harrison launched the "Hare Krishna Mantra" onto the airwaves and into the hippie culture. As yoga culture swept through New York and California in the 1980s, chant gained popularity. Krishna Das's melding of pop, rock, and gospel with traditional Indian devotions took hold in the 1990s, fueling modern kirtan popularity. These days, kirtan is an integral part of most yoga and music festivals.

Wonder-filled Wednesday

* * *

WEEK 2: SEE THE INVISIBLE

Alexander Calder's gigantic *Five Swords* sculpture sits in the fields of Storm King Art Center, nestled among the hills of the Hudson Valley. Created in 1976, the imposing, yet graceful, structure is constructed out of steel and painted a bright orange-red. Calder is one of my favorite rebels. Sure, he may not seem so now, but in the 1930s he was downright revolutionary, inventing the art mobile: a wire sculpture of multiple independent pieces that rotate gently in a breeze or with a light touch. Today they're everywhere.

But his mammoth metal work does not, obviously, move in the breeze. Which is terrific, because it gives people the chance to do the exploring. As I walk around *Five Swords*, each step provides a slightly different perspective. Because of its 3-Dness, it is impossible to see the entire thing at one time. I'm just too small in scale. It soars over 18 feet into the sky and is around 29 feet at its base. So I give up on trying to see the whole, and focus on what I can see from each shift in viewpoint: What if I crouch down low? What if I step back? Look what happens when the clouds pass! Look at the play of light and shadow!

What I love about the Storm King Art Center—and frankly any sculpture garden or art museum—is choosing which pieces to engage with, and how to engage with them. Plus, with art, I don't feel compelled to have to explain rationally everything I am feeling or thinking. My husband is an artist, and I always laugh when people ask him, "What does this painting *mean?*" He'll often get a perplexed look on his face and be unable to answer. Not because the painting doesn't have meaning, but because the interpretation transcends words.

We humans are always trying to describe things using language. But when it comes to art—and by art, I include not only painting, photography, and sculpture, but also architecture, music, poetry, dance, and so on—words pale in comparison to the original creation. A gorgeous sunset photograph looks neat on Instagram, but it rarely looks or feels the same as the actual sky experience did.

It dawns on me that Calder's *Five Swords* is what divinity is like. I can never see the whole—it's just too immense, and I'm too small in scale. Instead, I interact with pieces, each one giving me a different perspective. We're all just moving around this thing, seeing it through our own individual eyes. Accordingly, we each have preferences. You may like the sculpture from the left side. I may like it from the right. You may want your spirituality to feel more grounded. I may want to be more transcendent. (And we might switch those roles next week.)

Spirituality is like art—there is a world of difference between studying it and experiencing it. Predictably, artists agree. Wassily Kandinsky said, "Color is a power which directly influences the soul." Pablo Picasso offered, "The purpose of art is washing the dust of daily life off our souls." These masters of the visual remind us that art is about more than what we see. Yet so often, we whip through life, spending only seconds looking, missing the opportunity to engage with the wonder. Especially when it comes to art.

Consider the Louvre. As the largest art museum in the world, it covers 782,910 square feet of space and contains 38,000 pieces of art. The National Museum of China is just slightly smaller in size, but its permanent collection includes over 1 million pieces. Closer to home, The Met in New York features more than 2 million items. When visiting, we speed through, glancing for a second or two at each piece, perhaps longer for the most famous ones. We miss the spiritual moments hiding in the paint.

Spirituality and art have been connected since humans started drawing on cave walls. Sacred art appears around the globe, from *thangka* (sacred Tibetan Buddhist painting), sand *mandalas*, Islamic calligraphy, Byzantine mosaics, and *murti* statues of India to the influential paintings of the Renaissance masters and rebelliousness of contemporary outsider artists.

Visio Divina (divine seeing) is a style of looking at art from a sacred perspective. Traditionally, this practice used religious icons, but many of us may not be particularly comfortable with overtly religious imagery. Growing up Protestant, I developed a discomfort around religious art and icons in particular. I just wasn't quite sure what to with them. Were icons the same thing as forbidden idols? Why did they seem to stare so intently at me? What exactly are you supposed to *do* with them?*

With some investigation, I learned that *icon* is the Greek word for image. Interestingly, icons are "read" rather than "viewed," since they usually illustrate a piece of a sacred book. Thus, an icon is a visual interpretation of sacred words. Icon painters are trained through lineages, learning specific symbols, figures, and styles. In traditional icons, there is not a particular light source—so you won't see shadows. Instead, the light permeates the entire piece, suggesting the uncreated light of divinity. Usually the focal point is a face, with eyes designed to gaze at you, as you look back. The mouths are closed, inviting us to stare in silence.

The goal of Visio Divina is not to be just a drive-by art viewer, but to build a relationship with the image through meditative gazing. This practice can be expanded way beyond traditional religious icons, of course. Art museums, sculpture gardens, and illustrated books can be excellent places to engage in a sacred moment.

For example, in his stunning art book *Yoga: The Secret of Life*, Francesco Mastalia captures a mystical state of being through the 19th-century labor-intensive—and incredibly fragile—photography technique known as the collodion process. His antique camera is a sight to behold, standing tall on three legs, made from gorgeous wood framing a black, expanding accordion. The process begins by pouring an emulsion and light-sensitive salts onto a sheet of black glass. Rather ceremonially, the plate is then bathed in a solution of silver nitrate to render it sensitive to light. The plate is then inserted into the camera; with the subject holding perfectly still, the lens cap is carefully removed from the antique brass lens, and the plate is exposed to light for up to 10 seconds. Next, the glass plate is developed. Originally appearing as a negative, the plate is immersed into a fixing solution, and as it clears, the image magically comes to life.

Through this intricate process, Francesco's incredible photographs are not just instant snaps, they are sacred art. Since the light exposure is longer than that of our ultra-fast modern cameras, collodion-process images capture the play of light, matter, and motion in a distinctive way. It's as if a twinkling of divinity has been caught—the invisible made visible. Francesco suggests, "The charismatic force of the collodion process propels us into the union of a known and unknown world."

Francesco described for me why he thinks this is: "The world is constantly moving, nothing is ever stopped. In the origins of photography, they always used time to capture an image. And now we just use a fraction of a second. We're just freezing a moment in time, and so we're unable to capture the energy that takes place over a 10-second exposure." Eventually, our conversation headed towards the metaphysical: "Light is energy," Francesco told me. "There's energy coming from the sun, which comes down to the Earth, which I feel comes through the subject, which comes through my lens onto the glass plate through me to the person who is viewing it. And it is all just one exchange of energy. It's the flow of life."

He hits on an important point here. Often, in the West, yoga is lumped into the category of exercise or wellness. (And I admit, I spend a great deal of time each day walking around in comfy "yoga" pants, which are honestly also my sleepy pants. The irony of that is not lost on me, since the guys who invented yoga didn't even wear pants.)

Though it is true that yogic poses can have amazing benefits for the body, the true spirit of yoga is connection to [x]. The postures use the body to prepare the mind for spirit. Francesco's work helps remind us that the word *yoga* means union and connection. In fact, for many who practice yoga as a spiritual discipline, the most important pose is sitting on your butt in meditation, connected to something bigger than ego.

So I wasn't surprised when Francesco noted that many of the 108 yogis and yoginis featured in his book did not want to be photographed in a challenging *asana* (pose), but rather in the act of yoga as spiritual connection. In my humble opinion, those photos are the most compelling. Rather than having the "Wow, that guy is super bendy!" reaction I have to the full-body photos, when I gaze at Francesco's close-up portrait images, I feel that I'm connecting to the divine energy coming through the sitters' eyes. As with our first Sangha Sunday practice, I get the feeling that I am relating to something vaster than me. I enter into a relationship with the subject, the photographer, and the energy flowing through the exchange, in visual union with the invisible.

Today, dip into the age-old practice of divine seeing, using your modern device, putting it to a wonder-filled purpose.

HOW IT WORKS

1. *Grab your phone or computer* and "silence all alerts."
2. *Close your eyes for a moment* and tune in to the flow of life force within yourself. Breathe to get your flow going. Recall Week 1's Mindful Monday gazing.
3. *Go to spiritual-rebel.com/visio.*
4. *Select an image* from the links list.
5. *Gently direct your gaze to the image*, which will serve as your icon for today.
6. *Approach the figure with reverence and openheartedness*, and gaze upon it in silent meditation.
7. *Next, explore the icon.* Move your eyes around for a while. Focus on different parts. Alternate between softening your gaze and sharpening it. Look for the invisible.
8. *When your practice feels complete,* close your eyes and sit for a few more moments in silence.
9. *Record any reflections or aha!s.* Note how your mind and body feel.

REBELLIOUS VARIATIONS

Get into the groove: Add some *Audio Divina* to your gazing, recycling yesterday's kirtan hits or a favorite track from your music collection.

Art immersion: Head out to an art museum. Give yourself permission to spend an obscene amount of time in front of any single piece. You may even vicariously impact those around you to slow down (and get a bonus chat from that nice security guard).

Go outrageously orthodox: Check out local religious stores or scour Etsy for a classically-styled icon. On a recent trip to Greece, I visited a studio. Passing by Jesus, Mary, and an inexhaustible pile of saints, I found one of my favorite badasses: Mary Magdalene. Clearly, I've overcome any early Protestant icon angst, as she sits on a shelf in my writing den.

Make it personal: Draw or paint your own sacred image. Consider people who have been influential in your life. New Mexico iconographer Fr. William Hart ("Bill") McNichols includes in his portfolio contemporary saints such as LGBTQ+ movement inspiration Matthew Shepard and peace activists Philip and Daniel Berrigan. And very close to home (actually *in* my house), Sean Bowen creates figurative pop-art portraits of iconic people who have influenced his own journey, including Black Elk, Bob Dylan, and Martin Luther King Jr. (And he painted me a damn fine Princess Leia that I like to pretend is my portrait.)

DISCOVER DEEPLY

- Read *Yoga: The Secret of Life* by Francesco Mastalia.
- Take an iconography writing workshop.
- Read *Image to Insight: The Art of William Hart McNichols* by John D. Dadosky and William Hart McNichols.

- Read *Mother of God Similar to Fire* by Mirabai Starr and William Hart McNichols.
- Watch Ron Fricke's *Samsara* documentary chockfull of stunning sacred art and architecture from around the globe.
- Read *Walking on Water: Reflections on Faith and Art* by Madeline L'Engle.

NOTES

* For those of you who struggle with the terms *idols* and *icons*, note that we are not engaging in this exercise to worship the images that we are gazing upon. Instead, we use the images as pointers for connecting with something deep within or that which we consider greater than ourselves.

Trekking Thursday

* * *

WEEK 2: NOT ALL THOSE WHO WANDER ARE LOST*

"It's a quote from the Buddha in Jedi script," I answer for what seems like the gazillionth time. It's my standard answer when someone asks about the tattoo on my right bicep. Often, I continue with a comment on how reading and hiking can be dangerous.

When I first started wandering where the Wi-Fi was weak, I had a hard time slowing my mind down enough to enjoy meandering. As an avid multitasker who struggled with just *being*, I needed to be *doing*. So I started hiking in the forest to sacred texts—sometimes by audiobook, other times carrying a book and stopping along the way to read. Unexpectedly, using both mind and body at the same time helped me embody the words in a way that was unavailable to me when I sat reading on the sofa.

One day, hiking to an audiobook of the Dhammapada (a collection of sayings of the Buddha), I stopped abruptly in my tracks. As I heard the words of verse 172, I knew immediately that they needed to be inked on me—fully embodied symbolically. I tweaked the words slightly and set them in Aurebesh (a writing system for Galactic Basic. And, yes, that's a thing): "*She who was once reckless but becomes balanced gives light to the world like the moon when freed from the clouds.*" It was an intense pointer towards my higher purpose. The words were simultaneously comforting and scary, as I suspected life was about to change dramatically. I could no longer ignore the spiritual baggage neatly stored away. An unraveling and unfolding of my dark secrets was about to begin as I sought riskier hiking routes and studied heavier texts.

As naturalist John Muir inspired us last week, so will Belden C. Lane this week. His Amazon author page describes him this way: "Some time ago he found himself delightfully introduced as a Presbyterian minister teaching at a Roman Catholic university telling Jewish stories at the Vedanta Society."** Plus, he's a self-professed recovering scholar who quotes Aslan (*"Further up" and "further in"!*), and a worthy guide for our journey further into the connection between nature and spirituality.

In *Backpacking with the Saints: Wilderness Hiking as Spiritual Practice*, Lane describes his chief reason for hiking as being "to let the mind empty itself, usually after a period of overuse." He notes that taking a saint along a trail is not an intellectual exercise, but rather like hiking with a Zen master, "having someone to slap me upside the head as may be required" to pay attention to what is happening around him. He adds:

> Spiritual reading can be dangerous ... the truly risky stuff ... haunt[s] us with the fundamental questions, overthrowing our previous ways of viewing the world. Reading a potentially dangerous book in a landscape perceived to be dangerous can

be doubly hazardous. The place heightens the vulnerability occasioned by the text. Challenging books lose their bite when they're read comfortably at home in a favorite armchair. Their riskiness increases however, when read by firelight in a forest glade, ten miles from the nearest road.

Lane suggests not only using the written (or audible) word, but also engaging in *Lectio Terrestris.* I suspect you get the gist of that term without explanation, but I'll elaborate for those of you not currently having a Latin-lesson flashback.

You'll recall that yesterday we experienced Visio Divina (divine seeing). *Lectio Divina* (divine reading) is a related activity, in which we don't try to study something, but instead merge with the words. People who do this practice formally usually follow a form of read, reflect, respond, then rest. Lane's Lectio Terrestris goes one step further, placing reading in direct contact with nature, to create "a richly interactive reading of the Earth itself with the expectation of being changed by what we read."

In the spirit of some spiritual multitasking, today we'll combine the two, intensifying our wilderness spirituality.

HOW IT WORKS

1. *Get to nature.* Step out your back door onto the earth. Or consider one of the spaces you found last Thursday. Perhaps listen to some kirtan on the way.
2. *Take some long breaths.* Do a little forest bathing or wonder practice to settle in.
3. *Slowly read the following words* from the Tao Te Ching.***

The Tao which can be expressed in words
is not the eternal Tao;

the name which can be uttered
is not its eternal name.

Without a name,
it is the Beginning of Heaven and Earth;
with a name, it is the Mother of all things.

Only one who is eternally free from earthly passions
can apprehend its spiritual essence;

one who is ever clogged by passions
can see no more than its outer form.

These two things,
the spiritual and the material,
though we call them by different names,
in their origin are one and the same.

This sameness is a mystery,
the mystery of mysteries.
It is the gate of all spirituality.

4. *Close your eyes for around five minutes.* Let any images or words float around without judgment or
   grasping.
5. *Gently open your eyes.* Reread the passage. Reflect on
   what you are feeling, what you have just experienced,
   or anything that is happening in you.
6. *See if a word pops into mind*, or maybe a short phrase.
   Listen to what nature may be saying to you. If nothing
   comes, try this prompt from our reading: "the name
   which can be uttered is not its eternal name."

7. *Write your word(s)* on one of the *Reflections & Ahas* pages or here in the margin.
8. *Now wander!* Occasionally bring your word or phrase back into your mind for reflection. Ask yourself: How do the words relate to what I see? What is my relationship to mystery?
9. *Rest.* After your walk, rest in a seated position letting the practice sink in.

REBELLIOUS VARIATIONS

It's just a phrase: If you come up blank, try one of these phrases for your trekking. Stop at intervals to read it, contemplating if the mean differs by location. Some ideas:
- *The idea of knowing exactly where you're going is overrated.*—Sarah Sze
- *Traveler, there is no path. Paths are made by walking* —Antonio Machado
- *There are love dogs no one knows the names of. Give your life to be one of them.*—Rumi
- *There is nothing new under the sun.*—Ecclesiastes
- *True humanity is within you. Seek and you will find it.* —The Gospel of Mary Magdalene
- *All things are in Nirvana, and it has been since the beginning.*—Buddha
- *Every little thing is sent for something, and in that thing there should be happiness and the power to make happy. Like the grasses showing tender faces to each other, thus we should do, for this was the wish of the Grandfathers of the World.*—Heháka Sápa (Black Elk)

Words of wisdom: Pick up sacred literature from a tradition you aren't familiar with.

- The Dhammapada
- The Upanishads
- The Yoga Sūtras of Patañjali
- The Tao Te Ching
- The Tattvartha Sutra: That Which Is
- The Torah
- The Gospel of Thomas
- The Qur'an
- The Egyptian Book of the Dead
- The Bhagavad Gita

Modern lectio: Check out these not-so-sacred-but-thought-provoking options.

- *Zen and the Art of Motorcycle Maintenance* by Robert M. Pirsig
- "Zen Parables for the Would-Be Jedi" from *The Dharma of Star Wars* by Matthew Bortolin
- *Traveling Light: Stories & Drawings for a Quiet Mind* by Brian Andreas
- *The Drowned Book: Ecstatic and Earthy Reflections of Bahauddin, The Father of Rumi* by Coleman Barks and John Moyne

The more, the merrier: Hike with a friend and stop to read to each other.

For the homebound: Assemble a tent in your backyard, awaken each morning with a sunrise reading or end each day with a sunset one.

For the citybound: Awaken your inner eight-year-old and build a fort. Attach a *Do Not Disturb* sign and crawl in with your book.

DISCOVER DEEPLY

- Listen to "Harry Potter and the Sacred Text" podcasts at harrypottersacredtext.com.
- Read *Backpacking with the Saints: Wilderness Hiking as Spiritual Practice* by Belden C. Lane.
- Read *The Solace of Fierce Landscapes: Exploring Desert and Mountain Spirituality* by Belden C. Lane.
- Experience desert spirituality at ghostranch.org.
- Read *Soulcraft: Crossing into the Mysteries of Nature and Psyche* by Bill Plotkin.

NOTES

* This line was taken from the poem "All that is gold does not glitter" by J.R.R. Tolkien, written for *The Lord of the Rings*.

** *Vedanta* is an umbrella term for a number of spiritual philosophies originating in India. The Vedanta Society was founded by Swami Vivekananda (a follower of Ramakrishna). Arriving in New York for the first World's Parliament of Religions, Vivekananda noted, "I am proud to belong to a religion which has taught the world both tolerance and universal acceptance. We believe not only in universal toleration, but we accept all religions as true." Concerned with both self-knowledge as well as the search for divinity, members of the Vedanta Society believe in a oneness of all existence.

*** The Tao Te Ching is a core text of Taoism, which has influenced not only modern Dudeism but also Confucianism, Buddhism, and Chinese philosophy. Descriptions of the meaning of *Tao* range from "the way" or "the path," to "the underlying energy of everything." Through a Jedi lens, the Tao would be synonymous with the Force. Of course, the paradox of the Tao (as noted in the reading) is that any description of it is incomplete, including these.

Fearless Friday

WEEK 2: SPIRITUAL BUCKET LIST

Every morning, our rescued goldfish, Picasso, watches in amusement as I throw money on the floor. With his head pressed up against the glass, he treads mesmerized as I ooh and ahh, hunched over foreign coins and an I Ching scribbling my morning thoughts.

For many years, Picasso and I have engaged in this morning ritual. That darn fish is near 10 years old, and I suspect it may have something to do with the energy we tap into. (The average lifespan of a goldfish is five to 10 years, but I have hopes for Picasso's longevity. Since the oldest goldfish ever recorded lived 43 years, I have some time to test this hypothesis.)

When I run out of the house "too busy" to cast an I Ching, my day rarely glides as smoothly as the days I do. Regardless of the effect on Picasso, it's evident the practice works for me. I certainly can't prove it doesn't. Increasingly, *can't prove it doesn't* has become an influential mantra. Rather than looking for certainty or proof, I rely on experience. As my exploration into spiritual experience expanded, I became willing to have a go at things I previously judged as odd, weird, superstitious, bat-shit crazy, or (less critically) not for me. Stepping forward with courage, I explored outside my comfort zone.

Since I previously threw the idea that "doing such and such will send me to Hell" into the sacred trash, I didn't worry about that particularly heinous result. (Or that any of these practices would lead me to the dark side of the Force or have me burned at stake.) But I did have some worry and fear nevertheless.

And that's not surprising. All of us are preconditioned to look for things to freak out about. It's the first thing a brain judges in any situation: Is there anything scary here? My answer was: Not on Fridays.

Instead, I chose to suspend fear, do something new, and strengthen my courage muscle. Giving myself permission to suspend all expectations of what a practice would do for me, I approached Fridays as experiments, with no attachment to what would happen. I started by making a list of things I was curious about. *Presto!* A spiritual bucket list.

At the top of the list were things centered around developing intuition. I've never been a fan of people telling me how to act based on *their* infallible scripture interpretation. Instead of seeking certainty in scripture, creeds, or dogma, I prefer to develop my own sense of inner right and wrong, based on personal interpretation and experience.

Enter the I Ching (also known as the Yijing or Book of Changes). This 3,000-year-old book differs from other sacred texts: It's meant to be interactive. Of the many translations available, I have collected a dozen, including Hilary Barrett's *I Ching: Walking Your Path, Creating Your Future*. Curious to learn more about working with it, I reached out to her. Barrett describes her path to Yi as haphazard and unintentional. After reading several versions of the I Ching and working with the practice, she said, "It gradually dawned on me that the answers weren't random, and this thing could talk. If speaking with [insert preferred spiritual being or absolute here] is this direct, this readily available, then perhaps the world is not quite what we thought it was." Sinking more fully into her relationship (and conversation) with Yi, it expanded beyond divining into writing and teaching. If you ask Barrett, "What do you do?" her answer will be, "Help people have conversations with truth." Notice she doesn't say, "To *tell* people the truth."

My own experience has echoed this, working with Yi isn't about sitting down and just reading the I Ching. Instead, I meditate on a personal question and then cast a reading. (There are multiple ways to cast. I keep it simple and throw three coins six times.) The result of the toss is a combination of open, solid, and (sometimes) "changing" lines, identifying one of 64 hexagrams. (Or, as Barrett describes it, "A six-layered diagram of interacting energies.") Each combo points to a part of the I Ching to read and ponder in relation to the question.

As my first morning practice, the I Ching helps me intuit the most important focus for the day and consider the best course of action. I Ching scholar Sam Reifler suggests in his book *I Ching: A New Interpretation for Modern Times*, "Ideally the meaning of the hexagram will have the feeling that it has been on the tip of your tongue the whole time." And that's usually the case. The answer is inside of me; I just need help accessing it.

On the table next to the I Ching is a deck of tarot cards gifted to me by a dear friend, Vicki. I'm a bit leery of tarot, based on a bad experience when a reader told me a super shitty thing, took my money, and sent me on my way. But I hate not to use a gift, so each morning I draw one card from the deck and check out the description in the little booklet that came with it.

I have many friends who swear tarotology* is a helpful, intuitive practice. So as I started this chapter, I realized it was time to examine my baggage: Could I approach tarot intuition and divination without superstition? To find out, I contacted Brooklyn-based Lindsay Mack, an intuitive healer, holistic counselor, tarot reader, and founder of *Tarot for the Wild Soul*.

Lindsay had me at hello. Since her journey has included a wide range of traditions (Catholicism, Wicca, and the teachings of the Buddha via Tara Brach), the words she used were inclusive, approachable, and not nearly as esoteric as I had presumed. Describing tarot as a language for spiritual connection, Lindsay describes her work with others as "aligning people with their highest truth. We gently detangle any threads of confusion or contraction that you may be experiencing, liberating you from panic, trauma, past pain, and resistance. These sessions are powerful unblocking experiences, delivered with warmth, kindness, and the occasional F bomb." (Clearly, this is a much different approach from my past traumatic tarot experience.)

As Lindsay continued to shed light on the practice for me, she skimmed the realm of neuroscience, offering an intriguing illustration: Every human being is born with two dueling radio stations. The consistently louder of the two is the primal part, its primary directive to keep us alive. Lindsay suggests tarot can help lower the volume on Station 1, so we can more clearly hear Station 2:

> When we go through life, we incur all different kinds of neural pathways, triggers, self-protective mechanisms, and that's related to Station 1. And because it's louder, we think it's the truth. Tarot can help sort out where people are getting confused because they are not hearing their second radio station, which is their channel and their truth. Essentially when

we are utilizing tarot in this way, for healing and for reclaiming, then we are talking about evolution. Let's say the first radio station says, "Stay at home, stay at home, stay at home," but the soul desires to leave and go out and visit Paris. Then we can have all kinds of brain chemistry experiences about that: fear, terror, obsessions about bombings. Station 1 will do everything it can to try to keep us grounded because it thinks that any movement might be a threat. When we use tarot for clarification, we are essentially honoring the brain, seeing it for what it is doing, acknowledging it, and saying, "Thank you so much for keeping me safe" and then we are looking at the facts. In this example, the facts are that the soul wants to leave for Paris. So how can we hold space for the discomfort while still doing what the soul is asking for? And when we can't quite link all of that together in the mind—because Station 1 is so loud—tarot can help.

I was immediately ready to have Lindsay as a personal radio DJ, helping me reduce static and tune in to truth. But since it's unlikely she will come to my house every morning for a reading, I started dabbling in my own solo practice based on lessons from her online course. Now my fish watches me throw tarot cards on the floor after my I Ching coins.

Of course, what we feed grows. So shortly after I met Lindsay, the universe tossed shamanic practitioner Steven D. Farmer in my path. Though I was drawn to the name of his experiential retreat, *Spirit Animals as Messengers, Guides & Teachers*, I was clueless about the content. Over five jam-packed days, Steven led our group through a series of activities to get in touch with our "power animals." Through guided meditations, animal oracle cards, drum journeys, and chanting, I discovered and embraced Squirrel. Sharing stories of joy and grief among fellow participants, we bonded through tears and an almost ridiculous amount of infectious laughter. Until one afternoon when Steven challenged us to take on the persona of our animals, unveiling face paints.

You know that feeling when you reach the edge of your comfort zone? This was my moment. And judging from the looks on other participant faces, I was not alone. As we timidly approached the paint, our boisterousness was deflated. Tension filled the room. Perhaps old art-class traumas were smacking some of us in the face. Our fearless leader patiently waited, put on some tunes, and hung back, allowing us to work through our fears. As we did, a miraculous site appeared. Jeanette transformed into a colorful parrot, while Steve's silver hair framed his newly painted white polar bear face. Dark as the night, Elaine's raven eyes peered at Connie's round open owl eyes just under her bangs. Wild and thick, Pam's lion mane framed her smiling face. Next to me, Laura's fishy face shimmered with beautiful azure and emerald scales. Denise's otter whiskers twitched as she giggled, holding a rock to her chest (for opening clams, she announced). With courage, I ratted my hair up into a squirrely pile using an absurd amount of bobby pins. In the mirror I caught a reflection, and promptly lost it in laughter as I glimpsed Amy in full Hanuman-inspired monkey regalia, a black yoga strap tied around her waist for a tail. Deciding I was all in, I grabbed the face paint.

No longer out of our comfort zone, our pod banded together to face the public, marching straight up to the dining hall, inspiring confusion in those we passed, as well as a deep love for each other. Months after the retreat, I still pull an animal oracle card every morning for a bit of inspired guidance. (I swear Picasso swims faster in his bowl every time I draw the Fish card.)

As unique beings, we each come to this book with a different history of experiences. So if you were raised on tarot, maybe sweat lodging makes your spiritual bucket list instead. Or Sufi whirling, dream work, or balancing your chakras. The source of our spiritual moments is limitless; we just need to use our intuition to tap in to lower the volume on Station 1, so we can hear what is being whispered to us on Station 2.

HOW IT WORKS

1. *Silence* your phone, computer, or anything around you that might ring, ding, or vibrate.
2. *Gently close your eyes.*
3. *Pay attention to your breath.* Notice your belly rising and falling, the movements in your chest. Perhaps add a big cleansing yawn.
4. *Become aware of your thoughts.* Notice which seem to be broadcast by Station 1 ("I have nothing clean to wear." "I need to pay the electric bill." "What's for dinner?"). Visualize a volume control floating to the left of you and turn it down to a murmur.
5. *Mentally change stations.* Visualize Station 2's volume control to your right. Increase the volume. Take a few moments to tune in to this channel.
6. *Ask yourself the questions below.* Record any thoughts on the *Reflections & Ahas* pages. Alternate between tuning in and reflecting.
   - What connects me to my intuition?
   - Where do I find guidance?
   - What spiritual practices am I curious about?
   - How can I make space in my life to tune in on a more regular basis?

7. *Explore.* Grab your phone or computer and investigate whatever topics or themes popped up. Create a spiritual bucket list of people, places, and things to delve into during the coming months.

REBELLIOUS VARIATIONS

It's in the cards: Although the Rider-Waite Tarot deck is the standard for card connoisseurs, modern decks span an impressive range of interest areas. From Steven Farmer's *Power Animal Oracle Cards*, to Lucy Cavendish's Japanese-inspired *Foxfire: The Kitsune Oracle*, to Yehuda Berg's *The Power of Kabbalah Card Deck*, there's an option for intuitive work inspired by most spiritual traditions and religions. After you choose a deck, pull a card (or series of cards) each morning to connect with what's going on inside you and how to approach your day.

Feel the Force: As Qui-Gon Jinn told Anakin. "Always remember, your focus determines your reality." In his book *Use the Force: A Jedi's Guide to the Law of the Attraction*, Joshua P. Warren offers tips for tapping into metaphysical energy from a spirituality-meets-science-meets-space mindset. In his Take Five visualization exercise, Warren suggests setting aside five minutes each evening to envision exactly what you want to occur. Write down the description using as much detail as possible with a positive focus. For example, "I am fortunate that my body heals more every day."

Listen to the animals: If you are an aspiring Noah, Jane Goodall, or Dr. Doolittle, dig into your connection with the animal kingdom by exploring their possible messages. Steven Farmer notes in his *Pocket Guide to Spirit Animals: Understanding Messages from Your Animal Spirit Guides*, "You can have a relationship with a power animal even if you're not a shaman or shamanic practitioner. One may come to you in meditations, visions, dreams, or shamanic journeys. It's a highly personal and specialized relationship with an animal spirit guide, one in which the personality and characteristics of the particular power animal that you've attracted to you is reflective of your own personality and characteristics." As you go about your day, watch for animals around you. Consider how their characteristics might be mirroring something for you to bring awareness to. After an animal sighting, reflect upon a situation in your life. For example, after seeing a bear, ask yourself, "Is there a situation in which I need to stand my ground?" A squirrel sighting could trigger: "Is there something I need to prepare for?" A hawk above could prompt you to consider, "In what situation do I need to focus on the bigger picture?"

Use the P-word: The simple six-letter word *prayer* causes many of us more trouble than all the four-letter words we discovered in our formative years. Others swear by prayer as their primary intuitive practice. Celeste Yacoboni's book, *How Do You Pray? Inspiring Responses from Religious Leaders, Spiritual Guides, Healers, Activists & Other Lovers of Humanity* provides 132 remarkably diverse responses, suggesting there are at least as many ways of expressing prayer as there are definitions of the G-word. Prayer does not need to be limited to speaking a set of words prescribed by a particular religion, directed to a specific deity. From art to poetry, to body movements, prayer can be any action that connects you to something greater than yourself. If you feel blocked about the P-word, consider how you might reframe your definition of it.

DISCOVER DEEPLY

- Take an online class from Soul Tarot School at lindsay-mack.com.
- Read *Animal Spirit Guides: An Easy-to-Use Handbook for Identifying and Understanding Your Power Animals and Animal Spirit Helpers* by Steven D. Farmer.
- Download Brian Brown Walker's *I Ching: Book of Changes* app.
- Read *Help, Thanks, Wow: The Three Essential Prayers* by Anne Lamott.

NOTES

* Tarotology, or reading Tarot cards, is a subset of the practice of cartomancy (which uses standard playing cards). Since its Renaissance beginnings, the practice of using cards was poo-poohed by Church leaders with wild cries of "the devil's work." People raised using the Roman Catholic *Catechism*, a guidebook for the faith, may be familiar with this direction: "All forms of divination are to be rejected: recourse to Satan or demons, conjuring up the dead or other practices falsely supposed to 'unveil' the future." Let me assure you, developing our own intuition is a far cry from trying to call up demons or start a zombie apocalypse. When using cards to tap our inner thoughts and desires, we are instead dabbling in the realm of Carl Jung's collective unconsciousness, working with the archetypes that underly our human narratives.

Seva Saturday

*   *   *

WEEK 2: DO SOMETHING FOR NOTHING

"Sarah, where is all our canned food going?" my father inquired one morning. It was my junior year of high school, and unbeknownst to my parental units, a flannel-clad homeless kid lived in my Ford Fiesta. (Let's call him "Matt.") But, alas, Dad was on to me with his keen investigative sense.

After several unsuccessful attempts to explain the enigma of the missing canned food, I eventually fessed up. Not surprisingly, my father wasn't angry. But he did suggest there might be better options for Matt than living in our driveway on canned food, spending his time skateboarding while the rest of us were in class. A shower, some clean clothes, and an interview for a dishwashing job followed. Matt moved out of the car into a cheap apartment and started on his GED. I wish I remembered his last name so I could track down the rest of his journey.

Indeed, my dad was no stranger to assisting the homeless. Never judgmental, he helped people connect the dots to improve their circumstances. I remember one guy staying in our church's boiler room for a while. Dad referred to him as "PIBer." The man had been caught peeing in the bushes (hence P.I.B.) by the local police, and my father had advocated for him to do odd jobs at the church rather than be put into jail. I'm not sure what happened to PIBer either.

Similarly, neither Dad's nor my actions in these stories were about long-term relationships requiring ongoing reward or recognition. They were moments of kindness and generosity, spontaneous acts of caring and connection.

Likely I learned this principle not only from my father but also from my most influential childhood teacher—the amazingly quirky, political, author/illustrator, Dr. Seuss,* who wrote, "Unless someone like you cares a whole awful lot, nothing is going to get better. It's not." (*I am the Lorax, and I speak for the trees!*)

Better is another hard word to define. It's subjective and relative. Better for whom? Last Saturday, I defined seva as "something done without any thought of payment, reward, recognition, or thank you." If I have a desire to change something, to fix something, to make something better, is it still selfless?

Honestly, I'm not sure, but I suspect the answer lies somewhere in the relationship between being and doing. There's a saying that goes something like, "Service is love dressed for work." Cultivating love, compassion, and caring is important. But without action, there are no trees in the Lorax's forest. Without effort, none of the pain and chaos in our world is going to end.

Which brings me to Joshua Coombes, a hairstylist from London. After a dark period of loss, he questioned who he was and what he wanted to do with the remainder of his life. Drawn to the feeling he experienced with people in his salon chair, he wondered if that connection could be expanded beyond his work. Then one day, he was chatting on the street with a man who was homeless. Joshua spontaneously offered him a haircut. He recalls, "That empty feeling I felt changed. The moment kinda turned on a tap, and this other kind of happiness started flowing in." And Joshua became positively addicted to acts of kindness.

Soon he began documenting each person's story on Instagram using the hashtag #dosomethingfornothing. Fast-forward just a couple years (and hundreds of haircuts). The *Washington Post* has dubbed Joshua the "globe-trotting hair-dresser who helps homeless people look sharp," but that's just scratching the surface, because his work is really about connection and dignity. About truly seeing people (who are often ignored) and listening intently to their stories (which usually go untold).

I recently had an inspiring chat with Joshua. Serendipitously, our call was planned for July 4: Me in New York, him in the U.K. Amusingly, I realized that almost 250 years ago our relatives would have been duking it out about the rights of individuals, struggling over how to *dis*connect. (Admittedly, the July 4 holiday carries mixed feelings for me, as I find that the celebration of freedom and independence can be a shiny layer over a dark foundation of war, cruelty, pain, privilege, and nationalism. But speaking with Joshua on July 4 was particularly meaningful. And shortly after our call, as if on cue, my Christian yogini friend Shelley phoned to wish me "Happy Interdependence Day." Deeper perspective, indeed.)

In contrast to our forebears, Joshua and I connected excitedly across the pond (and airwaves) on the topics of punk rock, spirituality, and what it means to be connected. He prefaced:

I don't come from a background of any particular religion or even much of a value system, per se, not one that was packaged up for me in any way. But I was very lucky. I grew up with a hell of a lot of love and I think that's the part I never overlook. I definitely went through a kind of atheist period. I wondered about connection and where that comes from: is it inherent and innate or does it stem from somewhere? Right now I'm in this point of "I really love people and I'm really interested in connection."

Through his interactions, Joshua offers time for people to *re*connect with what he describes as "their greater self, their spiritual self, and to the energy that is undeniable. To being awake."

But as the slippery slope of spiritual terms starts, I, of course, can't help but mention the Force. Joshua interjects, "You'll love what I'm looking at." He describes a nearby mural on the side of a Peckham pub: a spray-painted portrait of Carrie Fisher (in full-on Leia buns) with large yellow letters reading "The Rebels' Princess" followed by "Carrie Fisher | RIP | 1956-2016." You cannot make this shit up. Everywhere, connections abound if we are aware, awake, and open to possibility.

What I truly appreciate about Joshua's story is that it is continually expanding. He's not trying to hold onto a personal brand or keep the story centered on him: #dosomethingfornothing is an opensource approach. He's seeded a movement that encourages others to be included. When I asked him why, he replied, "I wanted the hashtag to be an open space for people. It's about whatever your thing is, whatever your connection might be to try and bridge something with someone else. I'm not a charity, I'm not a nonprofit. I want to keep this as accessible to people as I can. This is yours as much as this is mine."

As our conversation came to a close, I asked Joshua one final question, "What would you answer if someone came up to you and asked, 'How do I start?'" His powerful answer created the spiritual moment for today.

HOW IT WORKS

1. *On one of the Reflections & Ahas pages, write down three things that interest you.* These three things might be your passions, your loves, or things that you think you are pretty good at. It could range from music to embroidery to legal advice. Write down the three things that make you feel good when you are doing them.
2. *Next, write down three things in society that you're not happy with.* Homelessness? Factory Farming? Poverty? Illiteracy? Again, it can be anything.
3. *Think about the parallels of these two lists.* How can you do something in List 1 to influence something in list 2? Joshua Coombes asserts, "There *will* be a way to connect them. It may not come straight away but get them down and keep looking at them."

REBELLIOUS VARIATIONS

Kindness isn't always quiet: The late Joe Strummer of The Clash suggested, "Punk rock means exemplary manners to your fellow human beings." In this spirit, Joshua Coombes enlisted friends to create Light & Noise, a multimedia event of art, photography, music, and film to bring awareness to the issue of homelessness. Bass guitar player Mike Watt (of Minutemen and The Stooges fame), San Pedro-based punk rock band Toys That Kill, U.K. artist Jamie Morrison, L.A. artist John Park, and photographer Mikey Huff all stepped up to "amplify some of the people often unheard by society, existing in some of the poorest conditions in the United States of America."

A street person's best friend: Veterinarian Jade Statt walks the streets of U.K. cities with a backpack of vet supplies, from dog treats to antibiotics. As cofounder of StreetVet, Statt aids the four-legged companions of people who live on the streets (primarily dogs), noting "the bond between many homeless people and their dogs is profound, such that their pets' wellbeing is a life-shaping priority."

Helping street cats live all nine lives: In Athens, Greece, a handful of volunteers combine their love of cats with a desire to keep the city's large cat population as healthy and safe as possible. Without an office, shelter facilities, animal ambulance or transport van, or state funding, Nine Lives Greece feeds and provides medical assistance for nearly 450 cats who were abandoned or born on the streets. Their compassionate trap-neuter-return programs help keep cats—and their communities—healthy, as well as educate kitty "owners" about this potentially life-saving procedure.

Save a child from poverty: Australian philosopher and activist Peter Singer's short book *The Life You Can Save: How to Do Your Part to End World Poverty* proposes that as part of the global human community we have an obligation not only to the people around us but also to those around the world. No matter how much money you make, you can help. In fact, taking global wealth into consideration, if you make over $32,000, you are part of "the 1 percent." Take a look around your house and at what you have. Then ponder this: The median worth of adults in India is $608 in *total wealth*, according to a report by Credit Suisse, and the average wealth of adults in Africa is even lower at just $411. Making no changes in your life other than reallocating just $10 a week away from bottled water, craft beer, or lattes could indeed make a big impact, saving countless lives.

Employing the unemployable: What do you get when you combine Zen Buddhism, a no-questions-asked hiring process, and a love of baking? You get 35,000 pounds of award-winning brownies daily and happy employees. Greyston Bakery, based in Yonkers, New York, an innovative idea from the late Bernie Glassman, founder of the Zen Peacemakers, literally bakes for social change, with the motto: "We don't hire people to bake brownies, we bake brownies to hire people." Aiming to provide work for the hard-to-employ, Greyston allows anyone to sign up regardless of background. (If you've had Ben & Jerry's Chocolate Fudge Brownie or Half-Baked ice cream flavors, you've eaten Greyston brownies. And might I suggest Chocolate Non-Dairy Frozen Dessert with Fudge Brownies for any discerning lactose intolerant vegans?) The company's profits are used for low-income housing, daycare open to the community, a medical center for those with AIDS, and other projects.

Supporting recovery one cup at a time: I have a theory that every person is born with a certain amount of drink tickets. When they are used up, well, that's that. Some of us use our tickets faster than the rest of you, and find ourselves in church basements drinking a ridiculous amount of coffee. Frank Kerker, founder of Sober Joe Coffee, combines his love of coffee with his desire to put a dent in the epidemic of addiction. The resulting "coffee with a cause" raises money for sober living houses, is run by people in recovery, and helps to destigmatize addiction through in-store product demos.

DISCOVER DEEPLY

- Find inspiration or post your own #dosome-thingfornothing on Instagram or Facebook @ dosomethingfornothing.
- Read *The Life You Can Save: How to Do Your Part to End World Poverty* by Peter Singer.
- Watch the award-winning documentary *Kinshasa Symphony*, about the power of music in an environment of poverty.
- Watch the inspiring documentary *Waste Land* about the transformative passion of art in a community of Brazilian trash pickers.

NOTES

* Theodor Seuss Geisel, aka Dr. Seuss, didn't start out as the children's author through whom many of us learned to read. Originally an illustrator for *Vanity Fair* and *Life* magazines, he also spent a fair amount of time creating advertising campaigns. Ten years later, his first foray into children's books, *And to Think That I Saw it on Mulberry Street*, was rejected by over 20 publishers. After *Mulberry Street*'s very successful publication, he went on to author over 60 books, illustrate more than 400 World War II political cartoons, create The Seuss System of Unorthodox Taxidermy, and paint fantastic dark artworks with intriguing titles like *Cat from the Wrong Side of the Tracks*.

Sangha Sunday

* * *

WEEK 2: DO DEEPENING YOUR TRIBE

As I became increasingly interested in spiritual things, I quickly overwhelmed my husband. In true Trekking Thursdays spirit, I spent an entire summer hiking to different sacred texts. I'd come home—my speech zooming at 3x speed—to share all the stuff I'd learned that day, all the dots connecting to other things I knew, expecting, of course, that he would be just as intrigued.

For many weeks, Sean listened patiently, with an appropriate amount of "Wow" and "Cool!" utterances. Then one day, he was full, I guess, and told me, "I love you. And I'm interested. But seriously, you need to go find your people." And he was right. But I didn't know how to do that.

Technology to the rescue. I signed up for a meditation group, nature lover hike, book club, and (possibly too many) spiritual retreats. One day, I attended a lecture on Advaita Vedanta, one of the classic Indian paths to spiritual realization (I admit I signed up only because the name sounded exotic). The speaker was late. Super late. And I started chatting with the woman next to me about my journey, mentioning recent online classes and a burgeoning need to be connected to people in real life. I bashfully admitted thoughts of enrolling in an academic program to study spirituality further. When I mentioned the program name, she revealed she was on the staff. I loudly blurted out, "No shit!" which seemed to resonate forever through the quiet yoga studio.

A few weeks later, I enrolled. On the first day of the program, I remember simultaneously thinking "I've found my people" and "No one here likes me." It was as if I was transported back in time to the first day of junior high school, an insecure 12-year-old.

Fast-forward, and I can confidently state that I have found many of *my people* (much to Sean's delight). True, I didn't find one group that perfectly fit my needs. My people are spread across many spaces and places, which sometimes, but not always, overlap. It's a motley sangha for sure: spiritual rebels, light-workers, Earth warriors, spiritual gangsters, peace warriors, spirit junkies, sacred healers, and yes, even a few pious religious folks and a couple of atheists. I went from being religion-phobic to belonging to an expansive spiritual tribe that transcends any particular building or specific religion.

Auspiciously, the lady from the lecture, Robin, eventually became a cherished mentor. Once, when thanking her for getting me started, I voiced gratitude for these flourishing relationships. She offered, "You find the people you can mud wrestle with—metaphorically. The people you can get in there with and companion down to the depths of one's beingness." (Or, as I like to irreverently translate: get in there and get dirty with!)

Robin's comment reminded me that spirituality is not always bliss, love, peace, and rainbows. I don't only need mere acquaintances, or an impressive group of followers on social media. Sure, those are nice to have. But I also need deep friendships and a strong support network. Author Anne Lamott, in her book *Plan B: Further Thoughts on Faith*, elaborates on this idea, "One secret of life is that the reason life works at all is that not everyone in your tribe is nuts on the same day."

My friend Sarah Matteo took a smart tack to gather people after a loss, life upheaval, and move to a new state. Wanting to avoid becoming isolated or sinking too far down into the hole that is grief, she set off on an ambitious, creative project: to meet people and collect their stories. To start, Sarah printed up small cards. Whenever she met someone she wanted to find out more about, she struck up a short conversation and handed out a card. On the front were the words "I'm so glad we met!" On the flipside was an explanation: "Hi, Person: Based on my unproven impressions of you and the nature of our random or fated encounter, I believe you have a story to tell that I want to know about. I'm directing a creative project and I'd like to interview you. Please get in touch." A link to her contact info and website followed.

Sarah met with anyone who contacted her, buying them a cup of coffee or tea. Each time, she started the conversation with one simple sentence: *Tell me about your journey.* "I wasn't looking for money or some sort of validation," she told me. "I didn't want to impress people or meet people to sleep with. I didn't want to make business connections. I was coming from a place of curiosity, and just found that people really want to be heard."

This thought prompted a big aha! for me. Countless interactions are about being seen. In fact, I'll go out on a limb and say we might just be the most visually documented people in history. Each social media platform has increased the prominence of imagery, with words taking a back seat. Images (and videos) are filtered, edited, and altered to put our best look forward:

Does it fit my style? Does it support my personal brand? Is my lighting okay?

Algorithms step in to decide what we see in our feeds, determining who we will see and how frequently we will see them. We can quickly begin to chase our tails trying to figure out how to best be seen by presenting what people most like, letting other people's opinions weigh more heavily than our own. Even our apps for connecting—for friends or hookups—ask us to filter our preferences, assuming we know what traits are perfect for us.

Although Sarah is likely choosing the people she interacts with based on some internal filters (conscious or unconscious), she told me she sought random encounters. "Everyone is a messenger," she stated. I agreed and added, "Through inspiration rather than algorithm!"

Some of Sarah's chance encounters were single occurrences, stories collected in moments to treasure. Others have led to lifelong friendships. Through her curiosity, creativity, and holy listening, Sarah connected and deepened her tribe.

Today take a depth check on yours.

HOW IT WORKS

1. *Close your eyes and visualize* a couple of interactions with your people.
2. *Ask yourself* these questions, waiting for an honest answer from within yourself:
   - How often am I fully present, giving people 100 percent of my attention (instead of multi-tasking or staring at a screen)?
   - Do my relationships feel balanced regarding terms of giving and receiving?

- Do I respect people with views that differ from mine?
- Am I trustworthy? Do I keep confidences?
- Am I comfortable with growth and change in my relationships?

3. *Feel the answers.* Connect with how they feel physically, emotionally, spiritually, and energetically.
4. *Take some breaths.* Inhale and exhale slowly.
5. *Now ask these questions:*
   - Does anything feel lacking in my relationships/groups?
   - Are there any people I've met that I'd like to connect more with?
   - Is there anything blocking me from getting to know people more deeply?
   - Are there any relationships/groups in which I feel more nourished or nurtured?
   - Are there any relationships/groups with whom I'd like to spend more time?
   - Are there any people that I might benefit from spending less time with?
6. *Take another breath.* Inhale and exhale slowly.
7. *Jot down any ahas* about future actions you might like to take as a result of these reflections.

REBELLIOUS VARIATIONS

Call someone you've never actually spoken to: Texting, messaging, and emailing have edged out phone conversations. Yet sometimes voice-to-voice interactions can help heighten the connection, as you focus on a single sense: hearing. Call someone with no agenda other than to ask, "Hey, could you tell me your story?"

Text to know you better: Start a Q&A chat with someone. Consider one of these openers from Conversation Starters World:

- If you didn't have to sleep, what would you do with the extra time?
- What do you wish you knew more about?
- What's something you like to do the old-fashioned way?

Gather your tribe: Start a book club, game night, volunteer day, sleepover weekend, or destination getaway to mingle your people and get to know them better

Get help for overdoing it: If your drinking, smoking, snorting, eating, gambling, shopping, or sexing is bringing you more trouble than joy, consider joining a 12-step or alternative recovery fellowship for help.

DISCOVER DEEPLY

- Get probing chat starters at conversationstartersworld.com.
- Check out Eventbrite, Facebook events, or Meetup for group activities, causes, or communities near you.
- Read *The Social Animal: The Hidden Sources of Love, Character, and Achievement* by David Brooks.
- Watch Seth Godin's "The Tribes We Lead" on TED.
- Research full-time sangha living opportunities at ic.org.

WEEK 3:
Expanding

The deeper we move in the mystery of our soul,
the closer we come to hearing the beat of the cosmos;
and the more we expand our awareness into the vastness of the universe,
the closer we come to knowing the unbounded Presence
at the heart of our being and every being.
... the microcosm and the macrocosm are one.

JOHN PHILIP NEWELL

* * *

You were formed out of stardust.

Sure, your parents had something to do with it. But 99 percent of what makes your body was formed initially in the heart of a star.

When you were born, you had no idea you were separate, no sense of yourself as an individual. You didn't even know your feet were yours. In fact, it took a few months before you realized you were an individuated being. As you grew, you were taught how to be an independent, how to be *you*. Learning words, ideas, and concepts your sense of self evolved as you chopped the allness you once felt into youness and otherness. And you might have rejected some of the people around you based on this perceived otherness, which was too different from your youness.

Much of the spiritual journey is digging back through the youness to that space beneath everything you think of as you. The beingness beneath the sense of self. Although parts of you may change—your height, weight, hair color, likes, dislikes—there is a spiritness that remains.

Paradoxically, that youness is part of the allness. Nine out of 10 people I polled agree: from a spiritual perspective, there is no otherness. (There's always one guy who goes against the grain.)

Everything is interbeingness. You are the allness, the isness, the oneness. You are not only [insert your name here], you are *that*.

Hold on to your hats—or your space helmets?—my friends. This week, I invite you to stretch into spiritual movements, ask a bunch of profound questions, and expand your perspective even further.

Mindful Monday

* * *

WEEK 3: ENJOY THE SILENCE

For me, the first gateway to experiencing allness is silence. In fact, I admit and proclaim I just spent an hour in a massive chamber drenched in eucalyptus scent called *The Green Steam* before writing this section. Because sometimes I must take drastic measures to get silent.

I knew I needed to because the thoughts in my mind were coming too fast and too furious for any real clarity to be present. In my life, I've tried several things to relieve this state—always outside of myself. Good wine worked for a while until it didn't. Escaping into a riveting postapocalyptic movie sometimes works. Spa visits soothe my mind, but often rip a hole in my wallet. Fortunately, when I learned to go inside of myself—with the help of silence—I found a free, accessible, source of calm. In his book *Seeking Silence: Exploring and Practicing the Spirituality of Silence*, the late Anthony Strano illuminated this sublimely. "When we are surrounded by a world of sound, we are not always aware of all the noise we generate inside our minds," Strano wrote. "Silence helps us to tap into the neglected spiritual reality of the self—an invisible but dynamic reality that flows inside each one of us." (Although *Seeking Silence* is currently out of print, it's worth finding a used copy or reading it on Kindle.)

But silence can be scary if we're not used to it. After signing up for a silent meditation retreat, I freaked out. How was I going to avoid talking for four entire days? Wouldn't it be boring? A waste of time? I thought I must be nuts for thinking I could do that.

Surprisingly, as the retreat started, my jitters began to ease, a sense of serenity came over me, and I felt chill. True, I cheated a couple times. I asked my roommate where the hairdryer was (she couldn't understand my pantomime on the topic). Automatically, I yelled *Gesundheit* across the silent lunchroom, when someone sneezed. And I called my husband-then-boyfriend once. Okay, maybe twice. Definitely not more than three times.

The point of this (lengthy) confession is to assure you that if you've never intentionally tried getting silent, 1) it is possible, and 2) don't be too hard on yourself in the process. Our world is increasingly noisy. Everything pings, dings, and rings. Our subways, cars, and planes talk to us. Our elevators, restaurants, bars—and even spas—have background music. We leave the TV or music on "for noise." When leaving the house, in go the earbuds or on go the headphones.

The silence we're going to search for today is not the absence of sound. It's not the absolute quiet of solitary or an institutional padded room. We're looking for the sound of natural silence. (Don't get me wrong, I *love* technology and tunes. But I also appreciate the natural quiet that occurs when they are absent.)

By stopping our own personal noise, we can hear more clearly what is going on around us. When we stop using our mouths, our minds can focus on other things—rather than "What am I going to say next? Aren't I clever?" Once we are silent, we become still in mind. And from this place of stillness, we can be aware and at ease.

Entering silence through the door of mindfulness can be helpful. By tuning in to where we are and what we're doing at each moment (rather than hanging out in the past or future), we decrease our habits of reactiveness and overwhelm. Removing the need to judge—or have an opinion on—things happening in our minds or around us, we learn how to live with equanimity. Think about your social media feeds for a minute. Each post begs for a response: a thumbs-up, a heart, a laughing emoji, a mad emoji. To be mindful is to see each moment of our life as it happens, but not feel compelled to react. Each minute in time just "is." Period. Not "is good" or "is bad" or a million other judgments we could make. Just "is."

Mindfulness can be done anytime, anywhere. Once you cultivate it, it becomes a skill you can whip out whenever you need peace of mind. It can even become the way you move through the world on a daily basis. Today our goal is not to shut the mind off completely, but to refocus it on awareness of the present moment, giving us opportunities to expand our consciousness.

HOW IT WORKS

1. *Silence* your phone, computer, or anything around you that might ring, ding, or vibrate.
2. *Still your body.* Let it rest. You don't need to be rigid, just still.
3. *Take a couple of slow breaths.* Sink into your surroundings.

4. *Gently say, "I am peace" aloud*, then sink into nonspeaking.
5. *Keeping your eyes open, look around you.* Unlike some other meditation styles, in this practice, we keep our eyes open to see, feel, and sense the environment.
6. *Observe, but do not absorb.* Let your thoughts roll by as if playing on a screen. Try not to attach to any opinions or judgments. For example, let's say it's raining outside. An observation is: "It's raining." Let go of any opinions ("I hate rain!") or judgments ("Rain is awful!"). Learning the difference between observing and judging takes practice. And of course, don't judge the judging. Quick tip: If the thought qualifies for an emoji, just let it pass right by.
7. *If your mind wanders, gently pull it back to the present.* If the thought has to do with the past or the future, just let it pass right by and repeat your phrase. Other options include "I am peaceful" or "I'm so chill." (If you want to get exotic, try *Shalom* or *Om Shanti*. Sometimes using syllables with which you are not familiar can bring a soft release of the mind.)

That's it. That's a basic mindfulness practice. You may find that you feel a sense of spaciousness in your mind that wasn't present before (which often expands with more practice). Perhaps you feel a connection to something bigger or something beyond. Maybe it just takes the edge off your day.

REBELLIOUS VARIATIONS

Silence your phone: Turn off alerts for an hour or a full day. Yes, the world can go on without you keeping track of it online.

If you worry about people not being able to get a hold of you, let them know beforehand. (Once, for a month, I left my phone off every Saturday in a self-created digital Sabbath—and missed nothing epic.)

I like to move it: Mindfully move through your day for an hour in silence. Go about your normal activities, but avoid words, opinions, and judgments.

In the car: Take a break from music in your car. Instead, take the time to be aware of the scenery around you. (And practice not scrutinizing other drivers!)

Cancel the noise: Do you live in a chaotic city? Have a long subway commute? Have chattering coworkers, a rowdy household, or a partner who snores? A set of noise-canceling headphones might be just what brings you peace. (I've been addicted to mine since first use.)

Clear your cache: Experience a blissful grownup nap time, relaxing yin yoga class, or enveloping gong bath.

DISCOVER DEEPLY

- Attend a silent retreat or meditation class.
- Listen to natural silence from Washington's Hoh Rainforest at onesquareinch.org.
- Read *In Praise of Slowness: Challenging the Cult of Speed* by Carl Honoré.
- Download Thich Nhat Hanh's Plum Village: Zen Buddhism Meditations app.
- Read *Living Presence: The Sufi Path to Mindfulness and the Essential Self* by Kabir Edmund Helminski.

Talking Tuesday

WEEK 3: THE KIND LEADING THE KIND

"Please do not take pictures to the turtles," I read aloud. Perking her ears up, my sister Amy responds, "WTF?" So I elaborate, "The hotel guidebook says we are not allowed to 'take pictures *to* the turtles.'" And I giggle. Flipping through more pages, I'm in stitches as I read additional rules to her, "Men are not allowed to use T-shirts." Then, "Do not take glass bottles out his room, an involuntary break in area of beach can cause accident, others manner allows the manager mini bar know." Huh? Next, I stumble on to this helpful information, "Neither the hotel is responsible for the actions of the authorities, popular rebellions, vandalism, sabotage, strikes, terrorism, invasion, etc." *Invasion*?? That's quite a thorough list.

In the middle of our snarky fun, I realize the only Spanish I speak is: *Si. No. Yo quiero una botella de agua.* And a sentence that isn't fit to print in a book on spirituality. Yet I'm sitting here in a ridiculous amount of judgment over someone else's translations. My impertinent mind jumps back in with, "Yeah, but this is a business and they *should* find someone to do this *right.*" Luckily, something kicks in and reminds me that one of my spiritual practices is Wise Speech.

This practice means I aspire to abstain from lying, malicious speech, harsh speech, and idle chatter. It requires that I acknowledge that words have power, and I have a choice of how I use them: to be kind or to tear others down. Although Wise Speech (or Right Speech) is best known as one of the elements of the Buddhist Noble Eightfold Path, the concept shows up in many spiritual traditions. My favorite is the Baal Shem Tov, a well-known Jewish mystical rabbi, who suggested we reflect on this idea: You were born with a fixed number of words, and once you use them up, you die. It's not a story meant to scare or shame us. It's a Jewish koan, asking us to ponder: How would you feel if the last sentence you uttered was, in fact, your last?

I'm sure I don't want my final words on Earth to be: "This is a business, and they *should* find someone to do this *right.*" Nor any of the other sassy things I uttered this morning, overtired from a long flight. That includes the story I told myself about how I compare to all the *other* people at the weeklong workshop I'm attending. Once the plane touched down, my amygdala jumped into hyperdrive, with my thoughts turning quickly to judge who is like me versus who is *other.* My spiritual sanity devolved into comparison, judgment, and gossip, moving from *all*ness to *me*ness. I am *this,* they are *that.*

Paradoxically, the workshop foundation was *Tat Tvam Asi,* one of the "Great Sayings" from the Upanishads. Roughly translated as *Thou art that* or *You are that,* the phrase is a pointer to unity: the Self in its primordial state is identical to the Ultimate Reality, the ground of being. Or another spin: You are like an ocean wave, coming into being, then returning to the ocean. We all came from something, into isness that is sameness with the oneness. Yet here I am, ego screaming, "I am special!" along with a bit of "I am better!"

It's not my fault—or so I tell myself—because humans are a storytelling species. When our words become memories, they become our narrative. Instead of being rooted in awareness and beingness, we can get stuck in the story, closing to what is unfolding around us. Our stories are rarely objective, instead, they are polished, curated versions of how we want others to see us combined with reasons we create for why things happened.

Which brings me back to the turtles. Present in many cultural archetypes, the turtle symbolizes longevity and immortality. Which makes sense, since turtles live a long time. Case in point: Adwaita, an Aldabra giant tortoise, is recorded to have lived 255 years. From Adwaita's view, I suspect the specifics of my daily stories would be inconsequential. *Please do not take pictures to the turtles.* Instead, let go of my story, my personal brand, my pictures. Speak to the turtle from a place of nowness.

Luckily, many wise sages before us have created frameworks for helping keep our speech on track: the kind leading the kind.

HOW IT WORKS

1.   *At various times during the day today,* before speaking, ask yourself the following questions (often called the Three Gates or Three Sieves):
     - Is it true?
     - Is it necessary?
     - Is it kind?
2.   *Adjust what you were going to say,* if needed, so that the answer to all three is yes. (Or if the answer to all three is no, think about zipping it.)

3. *Repeat.* Consider the same questions before texting, posting, commenting, or emailing.
4. *Reflect.* Jot down any tendencies on a *Reflections & Ahas* page.

REBELLIOUS VARIATIONS

Be noble: Use these guiding principles from the Buddhist tradition: It is spoken at the right time. It is spoken in truth. It is spoken affectionately. It is spoken beneficially. It is spoken with a mind of goodwill.

Invoke the Baal Shem Tov: Spend your day with awareness of what you say. Endeavor to make all the words you speak ones you would be okay with if they were your last.

Do "The Work": In her book *Loving What Is: Four Questions That Can Change Your Life*, author Byron Katie suggests asking the following questions about thoughts that trouble us: Is it true? Can you absolutely know that it is true? How do you react (what happens) when you believe that thought? Who would you be without the thought?

The Four Agreements: In the wildly popular book *The Four Agreements: A Practical Guide to Personal Freedom*, Don Miguel Ruiz proposes four guiding principles. The first is "Be impeccable with your word." How? Ruiz suggests: "Speak with integrity. Say only what you mean. Avoid using the word to speak against yourself or to gossip about others. Use the power of your word in the direction of truth and love."

Take it from Bill W., of Alcoholics Anonymous: When experiencing jealousy, envy, self-pity, or hurt pride, there is a 12-step phrase that can come in handy: "Nothing pays off like restraint of pen and tongue." When swimming in an emotional sea, it can be hard to speak kindly or compassionately. Sometimes the best course of action is to say nothing, do a spiritual practice, and return to the conversation when your head is back on straight. I find this phrase especially helpful when dealing with social feeds. If I read something that causes my heart to race and breath to quicken, it's time to exercise a little restraint of keyboard until I can come from a place of balance rather than anger.

Stop the Gossip: Before I met my friend Diane, I gossiped profusely but didn't know it. She defined gossip as "anytime you talk about someone who is not in the room." It's an intense definition, but it certainly changed my speech. For just today, try not speaking about anyone who isn't present in the conversation.

Learn Nonviolent Communication (NVC): Marshall Rosenberg developed a framework for compassionate communication that can be especially helpful in dealing with conflict and highly-charged conversations. Based on the idea people are trying to meet basic needs, and when those needs clash, we clash, the four-part process includes expressing observations, feelings, needs, and requests. If you are annoyed by your interactions with a friend or find yourself in constant conflict with someone at work, learning NVC may help you have more effective conversations.

DISCOVER DEEPLY

- Read *What Would Buddha Say?: 1,501 Right-Speech Teachings for Communicating Mindfully* by Barbara Ann Kipfer.
- Listen to the audiobook *The Four Agreements: A Practical Guide to Personal Freedom* by Don Miguel Ruiz.

- Download The Work App or visit thework.com.
- Read *Living Nonviolent Communication: Practical Tools to Connect and Communicate Skillfully in Every Situation* by Marshall Rosenberg, Ph.D.

Wonder-filled Wednesday

* * *

WEEK 3: HERE COMES THE SUN

Today my friend Charlie and I narrowly escaped being run down on the street. Okay, maybe that's overdramatic. But Charlie and I were standing dangerously in the middle of the road, debating the subtler points of spirituality. Again. For years we've been having the same debate, rarely agreeing on much of anything except our immense friendship. We are proof that it is possible to be warmhearted with people who do not share our same political or religious views.

"I have facts," Charlie asserts. "You have a perspective," I counter. He ups the ante, "I have evidence." Not to be outdone, I quip, "Your evidence is affected by your observer effect," invoking Schrödinger's cat.*

Fortunately, our debates are not always this polarized. Each conversation may start with us at seemingly opposite ends of an issue, yet we often end up realizing that we're arguing on the same side of the topic—just with different proof points and perspectives. One of our favorite items is the relationship between science and spirituality. We can go on for hours, on a circular route that never proves anything with 100 percent clarity except that we both like to talk.

Some of my other friends are not as delightful to debate with as Charlie. Another friend told me, "Science is the opposite of religion. In fact, science disproves spirituality; the two cannot coexist." I tossed some Einstein back at her: "Science without religion is lame. Religion without science is blind." Agreeing with these words from Einstein's essay "Religion and Science," which first appeared in the New York Times Magazine on November 9, 1930, I view each as a language to explain our human experience, able to inform each other. Both paths are ways that we humans document what is going on around us. And both can be "true." (Further, both views can also be subject to being turned into dogma.)

Science is an important part of explaining our lived experience. And yet, scientific theories are continuously redefined and superseded. Humanity has gone from believing in a flat single Earth to exploring an expanding (and accelerating) universe we are only just beginning to understand. As Sir Arthur Eddington (a contemporary of Einstein) famously admitted when describing atomic physics in his *The Nature of the Physical World*, "Something unknown is doing we don't know what."

The implications of that statement on what we call reality are profound. What we see, hear, taste, touch, or smell defines the perspective of our human experience. Or, as Morpheus says to Neo in *The Matrix*: "What *is* real? How do you define real? If you are talking about what you can feel, what you can smell, what you can taste, then 'real' is simply electrical signals interpreted by your brain."

When we start down the rabbit hole journey of *What is real?* one of the first stumbling blocks is *consciousness*. In his 1995 article "Facing Up to the Problem of Consciousness" (published in the *Journal of Consciousness Studies*), philosopher and cognitive scientist David Chalmers offers: "Consciousness poses the most baffling problems in the science of the mind. There is nothing that we know more intimately than conscious experience, but there is nothing that is harder to explain. All sorts of mental phenomena have yielded to scientific investigation in recent years, but consciousness has stubbornly resisted. Many have tried to explain it, but the explanations always seem to fall short of the target."

Chalmers observes that while research can now explain much of the *how* of human experience, the *why* is perplexing: "Why is it that when our cognitive systems engage in visual and auditory information-processing, we have visual or auditory experience: the quality of deep blue, the sensation of middle C? How can we explain why there is something it is like to entertain a mental image, or to experience an emotion? It is widely agreed that experience arises from a physical basis, but we have no good explanation of why and how it so arises. Why should physical processing give rise to a rich inner life at all? It seems objectively unreasonable that it should, and yet it does."

As modern science expands beyond a strictly Newtonian-based, cause-and-effect mechanistic view, an image of our Universe as a living system appears. And once it does, the question of *what is conscious* becomes increasingly relevant. Slipping into a topic which both science and spirituality seek to explain, I wonder about my environment. How far am I willing to consider consciousness permeating the world around me? Clearly, my cats are conscious, as are the mice living in our crawlspace. What about the trees in our yard and the plants underneath them? Where does the line between animate and inanimate lie?

In his book *Science and Spiritual Practices: Reconnecting through Direct Experience*, controversial biologist Rupert Sheldrake reflects on how spiritual practices can connect people with forms of consciousness beyond the human level—with "the more-than-human world." He suggests that because many of us have replaced living nature with mental abstractions, we've lost a sense of connection with the world beyond us. Sheldrake points out, "If nature is alive, if the universe is more like an organism than a machine, then there must be self-organizing systems with minds at all levels, including the earth, solar system, and the galaxy—and ultimately the entire cosmos." Many of us may be willing to go that far down the rabbit hole, but Sheldrake's next stop might not be so easy: "The sun sustains all life on earth. If we take panpsychism** seriously, then new questions inevitably arise. Is the sun alive? Is it conscious?"

Granted, Sheldrake admits, "As soon as you ask if the sun is conscious, you realize that you are violating a scientific taboo, the purpose of which is to stop us taking seriously what our ancestors believed.... I cannot prove the sun is conscious; but a skeptic cannot prove that is it unconscious. From a non-dogmatic point of view, the consciousness of the sun is an open question."

That sounds like a damn fine challenge, so let's pivot into a scientifically rebellious practice: wondering about the sun.

HOW IT WORKS

1. *Grab your morning coffee or tea.* Breathe slowly as it cools to a drinkable temperature. Yawn and stretch.
2. *Step outside where you can feel the sun.* Find a place where you can sit comfortably. Settle in. (If you missed the day in science class where we were told looking

directly at the sun can hurt your eyes, consider your-self now warned. *Feel* is the idea here, not *look at*.)

3. *Consider the importance of the sun to your life*:
   - Devoid of the sun's heat and light, our planet would be a dark, cold, ice-coated rock.
   - Absent of the energy of the sun, the plants that sustain us would not exist.
   - Without plants, there would be no oxygen for us to breathe.
   - As the heart of our solar system, the sun's gravity holds our universe together.
   - Interactions between the sun and our earth cause our seasons, drive our ocean currents, and determine our weather.
   - The sun has complex electromagnetic activity, some of which gives us the daylight we see by.

4. *Contemplate the following ideas*:
   - The human brain also engages in electromagnetic activity, as neurons communicate with each other through electrical changes at different speeds based on our activities.
   - These changes can be measured, correlating brainwaves with thought, emotion, and behavior.

5. *Ponder Sheldrake's musings*:

   "Most scientists believe that the electromagnetic activity within our brains is the interface between body and mind. Likewise, the complex electromagnetic patterns of activity in and around the sun could be the interface between its body and mind."

6. *Reflect.* How does this analogy land for you? Consider how this idea might influence your views about the

beliefs of our sun-worshipping ancestors. What is your personal view of the relationship between science and spirituality? Where do you draw the line (or do you draw a line) around consciousness? Is there anything else you find yourself wondering about?

7. *Note* any meaningful reflections on a *Reflections & Ahas* page.

REBELLIOUS VARIATIONS

Moonlit meditation: For some, it is not the sun, but the moon that inspires. Activist, attorney, and Wiccan priestess Phyllis Curott reflects in her book *Wicca Made Easy: Awaken the Divine Magic within You*: "Even though I lived in the midst of one of the world's greatest cities, I saw that the natural word *embodied* divinity. The Air was breath. Fire spirit, Water blood, and Earth body. Wiccan practices helped me attune myself—mind, body, and spirit—and come into harmony with Nature, with the elements, the seasonal cycles, and with the Moon." While the moon's wisdom and cycles are normally associated with women, Curott goes on to offer, "Regardless of gender, the lunar Goddesses also offer blessings to us all, which we can share and rejoice in together. And among these blessings is the magic of transformation, growth, and manifestation." So, no, you don't have to be female—or even Wiccan—to bask in the light of the moon. Its light is indeed available to all of us, regardless of gender or religion. Sit outside in the evening where you can see the moon. Gaze at it: Unlike the sun, this celestial body is safe to look at. Contemplate your relationship with it. Do its cycles affect your life? Or do you take it for granted? And if so, what other wonder-filled things might you be ignoring?

Ponder magical mysteries: "Magic is to religion as technology is to science," suggests Dean Radin, Ph.D., in his *Real Magic: Ancient Wisdom, Modern Science, and a Guide to the Secret Power of the Universe*. Radin continues: "Rising trends in science suggest that what was once called magic is poised to evolve into a new scientific discipline, just as medieval astrology and alchemy evolved into today's astronomy and chemistry. The new discipline will be the study of psychophysical nature of reality, that mysterious, interstitial space shimmering between mind and matter." Take a moment to reflect on your thoughts and feelings about the word *magic*. How do you relate to the unknown? To mystery? Or to things not easily answered by Wikipedia?

Dig into your dreams: The quandary of consciousness gets downright awesome when we look at dreams. In this alive—but clearly different—state of experience, time, space, images, actions, and even our sense of self becomes malleable and full of mystical symbolism. Then in a snap, what seems to make sense upon waking becomes a hazy remembrance just beyond the edge of our awakened mind. Is the waking state *real*? Or the sleeping state? Does each show us a piece of the experience of our reality? Do your dreams affect your actions? Place a journal next to your bed tonight, and just upon waking, reflect upon the dream piece of the consciousness puzzle.

DISCOVER DEEPLY

- Read *Science and Spiritual Practices: Reconnecting through Direct Experience* by Rupert Sheldrake.
- Check out groundbreaking consciousness research from the Institute of Noetic Science at noetic.org.
- Read *The Varieties of Scientific Experience: A Personal View of the Search for God* by Carl Sagan.

- Watch Tom Shadyac's *I Am*.
- Learn about Wiccan beliefs, practices, and traditions at phylliscurott.com.
- Read *You Are the Universe* by Deepak Chopra and Menas Kafatos.

NOTES

* In the 1930s, Erwin Schrödinger proposed his infamous thought experiment involving a hypothetical cat. He suggested imagining a cat placed in a steel chamber, along with a device containing a tiny bit of radioactive substance "so small, that perhaps in the course of the hour one of the atoms decays, but also, with equal probability, perhaps none." Thus, until we look into the chamber, the cat is simultaneously both dead and alive (known scientifically as quantum superposition). Schrödinger posed the question, "When does a quantum system stop existing as a superposition of states and become one or the other?" (In other words, when is it a dead cat or a live cat?) And can we answer that question without an observer, or do we have to look in the chamber for the state to be determined?

** Panpsychism is the belief that everything made of matter has some element of consciousness to it. This does not necessarily mean everything functions at the same level. So, for example, Sheldrake is not saying that the sun thinks in the same way humans do, but rather that both humans and planets might be imbued with the same mysterious essence that we call consciousness.

Trekking Thursday

* * *

WEEK 3: LEAP OF FAITH

"So basically, I'm just going to run off the side of the mountain, and you can meet me at the bottom," I tell Sean. He gives me *that look*, the one that means, "This is not what I wanted to do this morning."

Let me backtrack and catch you up. At the beginning of my spiritual journey, I decided my path needed an *actual* journey. An epic one. Whether spurred by the tall stack of Buddhist books on the nightstand or the approaching birthday with a zero at the end, a nagging call eastward appeared. Waking up one day with a heavy-duty urge to go to Nepal, the planning commenced. Pouring over travel guides and websites, I designed a legendary trek starting in Kathmandu, visiting sacred stupas and spiritual hot spots, then culminating in a breathtaking parahawking adventure in Pokhara. Which brings us back to the mountain.

Developed by Scott Mason, the Parahawking Project combines falconry with paragliding, creating an ecoadventure with a conservation message: to raise awareness of the importance of vultures in the ecosystem (who are facing extinction). For me, it was an adventure in faith. Luckily, I didn't need faith enough to move mountains, just faith enough that I would land safely at the bottom of one.

Onward my husband trekked (on foot for five kilometers) to the landing site, with the conviction that I would meet him, eventually. I jumped into a car with some guys, bunches of gear, and an Egyptian vulture named Bob for a 30-minute ride to the summit. I was given a thick birding glove for my left hand and a fanny pack of raw meat (*ewww!*) to fasten around my waist; the guide then strapped me tandem to his front and yelled: "Run." As we caught the wind and took flight, Bob flew gracefully in front of us, showing where the best thermals were. Occasionally, my guide blew a whistle. This signaled me to grab a small piece of meat and stretch out my arm. Bob would land, eat, and hang out briefly before heading in search of the next thermal. After the flight, we landed, much to the relief of my waiting husband, though very ungracefully for me as I did not follow instructions properly.

Of all the things we saw on that trip—the massive colorful Boudhanath Stupa, a live riverside cremation, the rare one-horned rhino of Chitwan—it's the experience of flying that sticks with me most. In hindsight, the entire trip felt like a pilgrimage to that moment. The journey had been a whirlwind of emotions: wonder and awe from meeting holy sages, incredible sadness at the poverty I saw, tremendous joy from the interactions with people who were previously strangers, and the courage needed to try something dangerous. (None of which were foreseen in our meticulous trip planning.)

Scarcely three weeks after Sean and I returned from Nepal, we watched *The Way*, starring Martin Sheen and Emilio Estevez.

Centered around a 1,000-year-old pilgrimage across Spain, the movie is a tear-jerking portrayal of the 800-kilometer route to the shrine of the apostle St. James the Great in the cathedral of Santiago de Compostela. As the final credits of the movie rolled, I professed to my husband, "We must do the Camino!" Without a pause, Sean declared, "Seriously, Sarah. Can we stay home just a bit before we head out?"

To ensure that Hollywood wasn't pulling a fast one on me, I checked out Kurt Koontz's book *A Million Steps*. "The first third of the trip is for the body, the second for the mind, the third for the soul," Kurt offered. As I read through his journey, I confirmed that the Camino de Santiago is not for the faint-hearted. The trek is not simply traveling; the Camino is a challenge, often with a personal focus (health, cultural, spiritual, religious, political, and so on). And I wanted to step up to the challenge, so I promptly ordered more books, some maps, and a state-of-the-art pair of hiking boots.

But hardly any time into my "Camino training," Sean broke his foot, and it still hasn't returned to a trek-worthy state. I'm tempted to think his fall was to avoid the six-week adventure, but he's not a manipulative man (and he loves his Harley too much to break anything on purpose). It was just bad timing and poor balance. While I'm waiting for his foot to heal to Camino toughness, I'm living vicariously through my friends, including Barbara Becker, who stumbled auspiciously upon her Camino trip:

> One evening I sat in the garden of an Italian restaurant in Little Italy with my friend Viviana and her daughter, who were both visiting from Spain. "I'm turning 50 next year," I announced. "I want to do something big to mark it." Viviana suggested, "Like hike the Camino with me?" I replied, "Exactly."

The truth was, I didn't know much about the Camino at all, other than that it was long and that it was in Spain, a country I love, and I would be with my dear friend. We shook on it right then and there while her 16-year-old daughter looked at us with surprise: "Really?" Clara asked, "Is that how you do things?" That sealed the deal for us—it was our duty to show a young woman of the next generation how lifelong friendship works.

After planning her Camino for over a year, Barbara's father passed away from a long illness. Reflecting on whether to cancel the trip (and urged by her family not to), she realized, "I inherited my love of the outdoors from my father, who hiked at least once a week with his friends. Taking the trip would be a great way to honor his memory."

Barbara and Viviana walked 225 miles over 10 days during a beautiful September with bright blue skies and no rain. As she walked, Barbara silently recited the 23rd Psalm—"The Lord is my shepherd, I shall not want"—which her mother had said to her dad as he was dying. Thinking about the last words her father had heard before taking his final breath, as well as her own life in relation to the psalm, Barbara contemplated what it means to wander like a sheep does without a shepherd to keep it in line. She pondered the seemingly irreconcilable concepts of certainty and faith.

As the pair marked the end of their hike at Finisterre—a rocky peninsula, whose name means "the end of the earth," jutting out into the Atlantic coast—Barbara sat on a boulder, high above the waters in the fog, looking westward toward her home far away. Of the moment, she told me, "I knew it was time to go back and to be with my family. I knew I would be leading my father's memorial service. I knew nothing would be the same again, but it would all be workable." In her words, I heard certainty and faith working together in hope.

I would speculate that the most meaningful part of our pilgrimages is not the amazing location, nor the number of steps taken. The value is not in the photos or the souvenirs, nor even in the amazing stories and memories we might tell and retell after the journey. No, pilgrimage is about the inward journey, the change that happens along the way, and how we return somehow a different being than the one who left.

From this perspective, our entire lives are pilgrimages. Today our trek will be inward, as we reflect on our life's journey to where we are now.

HOW IT WORKS

1. *Assemble some creative materials.* You'll need paper or cardboard. Even a brown paper bag cut flat will work. Find something to write with, like markers. If you have some old magazines or newspapers around, grab those too. If you have a crafty roommate (or kids), raid the glitter and glue stash.

2. *Find a flat space to work.* Make it yours. Bring coffee or tea. Light a candle or put on some music. Nest. (If you are working with glitter, for the love of God, put down a sheet or something.)

3. *Close your eyes* and settle in to the space.

4. *Pay attention to your breath.* Notice your belly rising and falling, the movements in your chest.

5. *Now travel back to the first moment you can remember.* Feel it. Open your eyes and visually represent it on your paper. If you want to be literal, go for it. But you don't have to! Consider drawing the moment with

a shape or swash of color. Flip through a magazine to find a word or image that fits. Or work solely in black Sharpie. Anything and everything is okay.

6. *Add the steps of your journey.* Continue adding more momentous occasions. Think about any leaps of faith or challenges of courage. Jump back and forth between reflection and creation. (If something overwhelming appears, hit pause. Call a friend or your therapist to talk through anything that bubbles up. I once sobbed for 20 minutes over a remembrance of our awesome, wacky cat Max.)

7. *When your journey gets to today*, decide if there is a next event on the horizon you want to add.

8. *As the last step*, add an empty shape for the uncertainty of the future.

9. *Oops.* As the last *last* step, you might want to clean up.

REBELLIOUS VARIATIONS

Spiritual journey playlist: If creative projects trigger any art-class trauma, instead document your life journey by creating a playlist of tunes that signify influential moments of your life. Start with the first song you remember and end with the last song you heard this week.

Quotable quotes: If you're addicted to underlining or highlighting lines that grab you in books as you read them, journey into your favorite titles. Create a list of key quotes that have influenced your life from childhood (Dr. Seuss?) to the book now resting on your nightstand.

Poetry pilgrimage: Poet Donna Knutson, known affectionately to her readers as "the Poet Preacher," has written as a spiritual practice every day for 12 years: "My writing is my soul work. Without it, I bleep out and get too busy with the world." Having amassed thousands of writings, she embarked on a journey to create *Finding God on Mayberry Street: Seasons of Spirituality in Poems and Reflections*, a collection of poems organized into four seasons, accompanied by her own nature photographs. Knutson notes, "I love that I can speak through the beauty of poetry in a language that does not separate but unites and resonates within the soul of people." Follow her lead, and embark on a poetry pilgrimage, writing each day on this question from the book: "Where did you see beauty today?" (Or answer a question you hear arise from inside.)

Make your travel sacred: If you hear a call to pilgrimage, start a planning journal to a pilgrimage-worthy location, such as:

- Shikoku Junrei (Japan)
- Israel's National Trail (Israel)
- The Inca Trail to Machu Picchu (Peru)
- Mount Kailash Pilgrimage (Tibet)
- Pilgrims' Way to Canterbury (England)
- Char Dham (India)
- And of course, the Camino de Santiago (Spain)

DISCOVER DEEPLY

- Watch *The Way*.
- Read *The Art of Pilgrimage: The Seeker's Guide to Making Travel Sacred* by Phil Cousineau.
- Listen to *The Happiness of Pursuit: Finding the Quest That Will Bring Purpose to Your Life* by Chris Guillebeau.
- Read *Fighting Monks and Burning Mountains: Misadventures on a Buddhist Pilgrimage* by Paul Barach.
- Watch *Sacred Journeys with Bruce Feiler*.

- Read *Walking Home from Mongolia: Ten Million Steps through China from the Gobi Desert to the South China Sea* by Rob Lilwall.
- Read *A Million Steps: A Camino de Santiago Book* by Kurt Koontz.

Fearless Friday

WEEK 3: FROM FEAR TO ETERNITY

Nothing can bring on the F-emotions—*fear* and *fright*—followed by a loud utterance—*fuck!*—quite like the D-words *disease* and *diagnosis*. I should know, I've got the papers for both. I've spent weeks in bed, months homebound, and countless years healing.

Before I got sick, I thought health was finding the perfect combination of a nutritious diet and strenuous exercise (neither of which held much interest for me). Further, I thought my mind, body, and spirit were three different things requiring different care and handling.

When traditional medicine could not resolve all my complaints, I added so-called alternative medicine. Just like my decision to try out spiritual practices that I had previously judged as odd, weird, superstitious, or bat-shit crazy, I looked into healing modalities I had formerly deemed quackery, pseudoscience, or unprovable. I slipped into the space where spirituality and wellness meet, soon acquiring an entire stable of wellness support: massage therapist, acupuncturist, holistic psychotherapist, Ayurvedic nutritionist, spiritual counselor, and chakra balancer.

As one modality led to another, I learned (surprise, surprise) everything is indeed connected. My mind/body/spirit was influenced by myriad factors, not just diet and exercise. I went from heavily medicated to decidedly meditated and firmly motivated. Eventually, I moved from needing a lot of outside support to being self-regulated.

Which brings me to Dr. Deepak Chopra, who is often at the forefront of conversations about wellness and spirituality. An endocrinologist, alternative medicine advocate, public speaker, and prolific writer, he suggests we think of the body as a process—a verb, not a noun. What we experience as our physical body is not static but continually being transformed. (And here's a freaky detail: What you experience as your body is only 10 percent human cells and 90 percent microbial cells—let's call one Sporos!)

Deepak's formula for a balanced life: Wake up every day with the intention that you are going to experience a joyful, energetic body and a restful, alert mind. Cultivate the emotions of peace, joy, love, compassion, empathy, and equanimity. Experience lightness of soul. To achieve this, he suggests six pillars for human wellbeing: natural sleep, daily meditation, movement, emotional balance, a healthy diet, and grounding. About now you may be wondering what this has to do with spirituality. The answer is wholeness. Chopra notes in his book *Reinventing the Body, Resurrecting the Soul*: "Wholeness is the result of connecting body, mind, and soul. In wholeness you aren't divided against yourself; therefore the choices you make are beneficial at every level."

If we are only focused on spiritual matters, not keeping an appropriate level of care for our bodies, all hell can break loose. Healthy bodies help us be resilient in the face of fear, allow us to tolerate stress and *dis-ease*, and to live longer, more joyful lives. Healthy bodies create the strong foundation we need underneath our spiritual endeavors. Case in point: Have you ever tried to meditate when you were hungry or sleepy?

Many of us have an annual physical with a doctor to see how our body is doing, but how often do we take focused time to assess what condition our body/mind/spirit is in, and create plans for good self-care? Well, if you are overdue, here's the perfect chance for a quick check-in. These questions are not meant to shame us because we haven't met our goals or to be used in judging us against others. Instead, use them as a gentle inquiry: notice and inquire.

HOW IT WORKS

1. *Take a few deep breaths* to get focused.
2. *Turn to the Reflections & Ahas pages* and reflect on the following questions:
   - *Natural sleep*: How is my sleep life?
   - *Daily meditation*: How often do I engage in mindfulness or meditation?
   - *Movement*: How much of my day do I spend sitting versus moving?
   - *Emotional wellbeing*: How do I feel emotionally?
   - *Healthy diet*: How am I eating?

- *Grounding*: How often do I connect with the Earth's energy?
3. *Consider* anything you'd like to do because of these reflections, or if you are content with your answers.
4. *Go enjoy your day*, cultivating peace, joy, love, compassion, empathy, and equanimity.

REBELLIOUS VARIATIONS

Enlist help: If anxiety rears its ugly head, consider answering the questions with the help of a trusted friend, therapist, holistic health practitioner, or spiritual director. (Spiritual directors provide one-on-one guidance for those seeking a deeper connection with whatever their [x] is.)

It's a family affair: Start with each family member answering the questions individually. Then let each person share their success and challenges, highlighting places where support would be welcomed. Avoid judging any answers.

You can teach a dog new tricks: According to the American Veterinary Medical Association's *2017-2018 edition of the Pet Ownership and Demographics Sourcebook* 57 percent of U.S. households include at least one companion animal. Amanda Ree, an Ayurvedic health practitioner and team member of the Chopra Center for Wellbeing, suggests that because our animals share our lives so closely, they are as impacted by people and events as we are. Her "Six Pillars of Dog Wellbeing," include Dosha (an Ayurvedic classification), Food, Behavior, Body/Mind, Emotional, and Spiritual. If you share your home with another species, take a few moments to consider its wellbeing.

- Find a spiritual director at sdiworld.org.
- Read *Yoga Nidra: The Art of Transformational Sleep* by Kamini Desai, Ph.D.
- Download Kamini Desai's I AM Yoga Nidra app.
- Read *Perfect Health: The Complete Mind/Body Guide* by Deepak Chopra, M.D.
- Learn more about the "Six Pillars of Dog Wellbeing" at samadog.com.
- Read *The Healing Wisdom of Africa: Finding Life Purpose through Nature, Ritual, and Community* by Malidoma Patrice Somé.
- Read *Mother Earth Spirituality: Native American Paths to Healing Ourselves and Our World* by Ed McGaa, Eagle Man.

Seva Saturday

* * *

WEEK 3: MAY THE FORK BE WITH YOU

Buba-ji and Deacon are not happy with me today. They were intent on loving the meeces to pieces when I swooped in with Tupperware to stop the slaughter. As they meow and run frantically around my feet, I explain to them, "The Dalai Lama says, 'Our prime purpose in this life is to help others. And if you can't help them, at least don't hurt them.'" I swear Bub is rolling his big round cat eyes at me, wishing he could speak human to explain the mice are his dharma.

This divide between my cats and me is due to differences in ideology. Because as well as being an aspiring Jedi, I'm also an aspiring Jain. Based on living in right relationship with everything in the universe, Jainism is another ancient path of Indic thought. In his book *The Jain Path: Ancient Wisdom for the West*, Aidan Rankin describes two key tenets. First, *ahimsā* is avoidance of harm. People following the Jain path will go to incredible lengths in their diets and lifestyle to avoid intentionally harming any living thing.

Second is *syādvāda*, or the belief that on any topic there will always be many viewpoints. Often referred to as many-sidedness, this concept can promote tolerance, as well as remove the need to prove that any one side is right for everyone. Rankin notes, "Each mind is different and is therefore inclined to see things differently, according to its own perspective. So one should tolerate and even honor a diversity of point of view on any subject. There is no need to promote any belief ideology or philosophy as the only truth, the final truth or the last word for all of humanity."

Unfortunately, neither my cats nor I am ready to be full Jains. Buba-ji and Deacon are obligate carnivores. Without the taurine, arachidonic acid, and arginine present in meat, they are likely to get very sick and die prematurely. It turns out Bub is right, chasing small animals is indeed part of his dharma. (We've compromised: I still save the mice, he gets a special cat food I hope lives up to the humane standards the company proclaims.)

Although I'm not quite ready to make the commitment required to be an official member of the Jain community, I am prepared to apply these principles the best I can to my own life as a many-sided multi-pather.

I've always been uncomfortable with the concept that the Earth and its animals are here for our use in any way we see fit. I was raised with lessons on sustainability and humaneness, alongside societal rules about what was okay to eat or use, and in which ways. But the instructions were often in conflict with each other and confusing, especially when it came to the difference between the animals I was taught to love and the ones I was told to eat. Melanie Joy, author of *Why We Love Dogs, Eat Pigs, and Wear Cows: An Introduction to Carnism*, explains that we are taught to "think of farmed animals as abstractions, as lacking any individuality or personality of their own. This distorted thinking distances us from our natural ability to identify and empathize with these beings." We separate the terms *meat* and *animal* as if they are different things. Likewise, we divide the concept of *Earth* from those of *resources* and *fuel*. Busy with our day-to-day lives, we are often disconnected from the consequences that our seemingly harmless choices have.

In between Jainism and an I-want-it-all-and-I-don't-care-about-the-consequences attitude is a wide range of options. Just as we choose our individual spiritual paths, I believe people should also make their own choices about what they consume. But we often make our decisions without complete information or in denial of the knowledge we do have. Or we think our actions only affect us, and remain oblivious to their impact on other people, creatures, and the Earth. While researching this subject, I learned a lot of things I would rather not know, including the dark side to some of my own choices.

Yesterday we looked at how our decisions affect our body/mind/spirit. Today we'll look at how our choices expand outward. Don't worry, this is not the part where I tell you that to live a spiritual life you have to give up all your belongings, get off the grid, become vegan, and stop having sex. (Of course, if you want to do any or all those things, go for it.) But I would like to share just a couple of the things I learned which surprised me.

- *We currently use 1.7 Earths a year*: The Global Footprint Network tabulates an "Earth Overshoot Day" each year to bring awareness to the day each year when all of humanity will have used more from nature than can be replenished in a year, through overfishing, overharvesting forests, and emitting more carbon dioxide into the atmosphere than ecosystems can absorb. In 2018, that date fell on August 1.

- *We eat a lot of meat*: The average American eats almost 200 pounds of animal protein each year per person (more than almost any other people on the planet and nearly twice as much as our ancestors ate 75 years ago). That's 2,000 land animals for each person over a lifetime (and 9 billion animals each year in the U.S. alone.)
- *And it doesn't come from idyllic farms*: I spent many summers at my grandparents' place in South Carolina, which looked like a storybook farm, and where all animals were treated well (up until their death, of course). In hindsight, it skewed my idea of where meat came from. Currently, industrial-scale factory farming accounts for 99.9 percent of chickens for meat, 97 percent of laying hens, 99 percent of turkeys, 95 percent of pigs, and 78 percent of cattle. I'd love to tell you more about the inherent cruelty in this system and the health issues for humans, but you might lose your breakfast.
- *It's screwing up our environment*: Globally, animal agriculture is responsible for more greenhouse gases than all transportation systems combined. The amount we're eating is also not sustainable. Animal ag is a super inefficient use of land, water, and creates an incredible amount of pollution.
- *Switching to fish and seafood doesn't solve all the problems*: Because of commercial fishing operations, a lot of fishing now happens by huge nets being pulled through the ocean. Much of what gets in the net is "unintentional bycatch" and gets discarded. For example, for every pound of commercial shrimp, it's estimated that up to 15 pounds of other ocean life are tossed back into the sea either already dead or dying, including seahorses, fish, and even large cetaceans like dolphins.

- *Fruits and vegetables aren't off the hook.* Roughly one-third of the food produced in the world for human consumption every year gets lost or wasted. Although some of that happens before the food arrives in our homes, it is estimated the average person in the U.S. (and Europe) throws away over 200 pounds of food a year.

Okay, that's enough of a slice to make a point: Our choices matter. Humanity's overindulgence (whether intentionally or unknowingly) has us on a path that may lead to our own extinction.

So it's not surprising that many people are embracing alternative diets and taking stock of their purchases and lifestyle. Which brings me back to today's focus: *seva*. By far, the biggest act of seva we can give ourselves, others, our planet, and its many living things is to look at our habits.

But it's not an easy task, because everything has a cost, and no answer is perfect. For example, I'm not ready to give up my beloved white Jeep Wrangler (with its FORCBWU license plates), which makes my Prius-driving friends crazy. But when I explain to them that I offset it by eating almost no meat—while they are chowing down on a steak—we start to have a different conversation.

From a spiritual perspective, I try to bring my choices into close alignment with my understanding of the interconnection of everything. To ask questions, learn details, and make informed decisions. My goal is not to shame myself, nor to blame others, but to look deeply at what is, and see how it feels for me. Which is how I found the *reducetarians*.

Brian Kateman is the co-founder of the Reducetarian Foundation and the author of *The Reducetarian Solution: How the Surprisingly Simple Act of Reducing the Amount of Meat in Your Diet Can Transform Your Health and the Planet.* His message is simple: "The less meat we eat, the more animals we save. And along the way, reducetarians mitigate water scarcity and climate change issues."

Although Kateman's definition of the term deals solely with meat, I've found that expanding a reducetarian perspective into all areas of my life has provided a framework for living compassionately and more in balance with nature. I've named my practice *Spiritualtarian*, endeavoring to align each one of my choices with my spiritual values. Just a few results: I switched to cruelty-free shampoo and cosmetics, joined a local CSA to support local humane farmers, and started giving microloans to people in other countries to help them eat and have clean water. And I'm just getting started.

Today, take a few minutes to build on yesterday's questions about the state of your body/mind/spirit with a few about your daily choices. I call these "Goldilocks questions." As you might recall, Goldilocks was the hungry little girl who stumbled upon the home of the Three Bears. Wandering through their house, she tested their porridge, sat in their chairs, and slept in their beds, judging each along the way. (Too hot, too cold, just right! Too hard, too soft, just right!) Today wander through your own place, discovering what feels in balance and what might need a little adjustment.

HOW IT WORKS

1. *Take a few deep breaths* to get focused, perhaps add a short meditation or add a blessing for the Earth and its many inhabitants.
2. *Reflect* for a few minutes on what is important to you: Sustainable Earth? Animal welfare? Food availability? Worker fairness?

3. *Turn to the Reflections & Ahas pages* and answer the following questions:
   - *Kitchen*: How do I feel about what I eat?
   - *Bathroom*: What do I think about the products I use? How is my water consumption?
   - *Closet*: Am I knowledgeable about how my clothing was made and what it is made of?
   - *Home environment*: How do I feel about my home furnishings, use of energy, and consumption of water?
   - *Financial footprint*: Do I know where my money goes, how much I donate, and what any investments support?
   - *Online footprint*: Am I comfortable with the content of my postings?
4. *Throughout today, slow down your decision-making process.* Use mindfulness to make choices that best serve your values. Gently question your decisions, allowing room for new answers if they arise. Resist the urge to shame or scold yourself. These are your choices, and your own process.
5. *Consider* seeking information about anything that seemed too much or too little from your Goldilocks perspective. The Discover Deeply section below contains some favorite resources I found on my own search.

REBELLIOUS VARIATIONS

One day at a time: If the list of questions feels overwhelming, do one item each day (or each Saturday for the next month or so).

Strength in numbers: If the questions feel to difficult to approach on your own, gather a few friends for dinner and mull over the questions together.

For the decision perplexed: Read *Ethics (for the Real World): Creating a Personal Code to Guide Decisions in Work and Life* by Ronald A. Howard and Clifton D. Korver, with Bill Birchard.

DISCOVER DEEPLY

May the fork be with you:
- Watch *Vegucated.*
- Read *The Good Karma Diet: Eat Gently, Feel Amazing, Age in Slow Motion* by Victoria Moran for help aligning eating and ethics.
- Read *Eating Animals* by Jonathan Safran Foer for a fascinating many-sided exploration into today's farming and food industry.
- Help some of the 800 million people who go to bed hungry each night by redirecting a bit of your food budget to an organization such as Oxfam or the Global Alliance for Improved Nutrition.

Love your mother (Earth):
- Find ways to reduce carbon emissions and energy costs at carbonfootprint.com.
- Learn just how much water goes into powering your cell phone or making your sandwich—as well as tips for curbing your water usage—at watercalculator.org.
- Read *Taking on Water: How One Water Expert Challenged Her Inner Hypocrite, Reduced Her Water Footprint (Without Sacrificing a Toasty Shower), and Found Nirvana* by Wendy J. Pabich.
- Take the Order of the Sacred Earth vow: "I promise to be the best lover and defender of Mother Earth that I can be." Seventy-six-year-old spiritual theologian and activist Matthew Fox joined 30-something wilderness

activists Skylar Wilson and Jennifer Berit Listug to create a vision for sacred living steeped in deep love of the Earth and based on an accessible, common vow, independent of a specific building or community. Read *Order of the Sacred Earth: An International Vision of Love and Action* for more details.

If you love animals:

- Download the *Bunny Free* app to find out if a company tests on animals.
- Read *Why We Love Dogs, Eat Pigs, and Wear Cows* by Melanie Joy, Ph.D.
- Get involved in animal advocacy with an organization such as World Animal Protection, Animal Equality, or Mercy for Animals.
- Listen to *A Plea for the Animals: The Moral, Philosophical, and Evolutionary Imperative to Treat All Beings with Compassion* by Matthieu Ricard.
- Read *The Human Gardener: Nurturing a Backyard Habitat for Wildlife* by Nancy Lawson.
- Watch *Speciesism*.

Put your money where your mouth is:

- Microlend with Kiva. For as little as $25 you can help someone create opportunity for a better life.
- Run a check-up on the effectiveness of your charitable giving at charitynavigator.org or givewell.org.
- If you have investment accounts, check into what your mutual funds fund to ensure that they support your values.

Sangha Sunday

* * *

WEEK 3: SACRED SPACE CRASHING

"Are you looking for the Darth Vader?" I ask, peering out from behind my binoculars. "Yes!" the man near me exclaims, "Can you see it?" We're standing outside Washington National Cathedral in D.C., staring up at the northwest tower, looking for a gargoyle in the shape of Darth Vader's head. (Actually, it's not a *gargoyle*, which traditionally means a rain spout, but a *grotesque*, which defines a fanciful human or animal architectural form and is only decorative.)

You might be wondering how a fearful villain ended up here. Excellent question. In the 1980s, as the building's west towers were under construction, the cathedral held a design competition for kids. Christopher Rader's Vader drawing won third place, and Darth soon took his place on the exterior. Nearly half a million people a year visit the cathedral, which "seeks to be a catalyst for spiritual harmony in our nation, reconciliation among faiths, and compassion in the world." From that perspective, reconciling Vader seems to be a stellar place to start.

The visit is another stop on my never-ending pilgrimage to spiritually-charged locations. After my original trek to Nepal, I quickly developed a travel addiction, with a very full bucket list: Lourdes, Varanasi, Easter Island, Wittenberg, Uluru, and the list goes on. Sarah Baxter, in her gorgeously illustrated book, *Spiritual Places (Inspired Traveller's Guides)*, describes the experience knowingly: "There are certain places that manage to seep into your soul. They don't stop at delighting your external senses with their drama or design. No, they have a way of inching further; of permeating your skin and sinking deep, deep down inside; of making you ask new questions about yourself, maybe even about the crux of human existence."

When money was tight, I headed out in my Jeep to see America, guided by the quirky folks at Roadside America and Atlas Obscura. Soon I realized my escapades were more alive when other people were involved. Engaging with members of spiritual communities (rather than tour guides and camera-toting tourists) was much more captivating. As a self-proclaimed spiritual "free agent," my travels are never limited to any specific religion or denomination. Instead, I am led by words borrowed from British philosopher William Paley and American humorist Mark Twain.

Twain's contribution is from his book *The Innocents Abroad*: "Travel is fatal to prejudice, bigotry, and narrow-mindedness." Travel helps me see people as individuals, and to see the great diversity of viewpoints everywhere I go. Globe-trotting helps me understand people and where they are coming from in their opinions and beliefs, creating gaping holes in my stereotypes and generalizations.

Because generalizations bug me. Whenever I hear someone say, "Christians believe..." or "Muslims think..." or "Buddhists say...," I cringe. Really? Have you talked to *every* Christian? Or even a representative from each denomination? (The World Christian Database states there are over 9,000.) Likewise, there are multiple divisions in every religion I've checked. Not one is unified. Even within each group, individual views differ. If you are feeling resistance to this idea because I've used the R-word, try one of these: "Californians think..." or "Men believe..." There's just no way for these statements to hold up to scrutiny.

Which brings me to Paley, who wrote in his book *Evidences of Christianity*: "Contempt prior to examination is an intellectual vice, from which the greatest faculties of mind are not free." These words remind me that I can be very quick to judge what is not for me—to reject ideas, people, and places without examining them thoroughly, or based solely on some past snippet of info. For example, scholars estimate that there are 4,200 religions in the world. So it's hard for me to say "all religions are bullshit" if I've only ever experienced one, or the big five, or even a dozen. What I call "sacred space-crashing" creates the possibility that someday I might just stumble into the perfect one, like finding Cinderella's glass slipper. And in the meantime, I'm learning what resonates with me—and what doesn't. With each visit, I understand a little more about the people who hang out there.

By traveling to different places and spaces, my judgments about groups can be replaced by the authentic stories of individual people. Admittedly, I don't always agree with some, and occasionally I vehemently disagree. But instead of lobbing F-bombs at them on social media, I'm engaged in trying to find our similarities, so we can more compassionately discuss our differences. Often, meeting people from other religions has helped me question my own presumptions and generalizations. And occasionally, vice versa.

I've also learned that transcending the discussion of beliefs can be helpful. Increasingly, I'm keen on experiencing how a location, ritual, or spiritual practice feels for me, rather than being told what it is supposed to be about or do for me.

I've lodged with Lakotas; whirled till I dropped with Sufis; meditated with Buddhists; immersed myself in 12-step meetings; bowed my head reverently in prayer with Catholics; hit the floor solemnly with Muslims; chanted seemingly endless kirtan with Hindus; sung really, really loud in a Christian megachurch; davened quietly with Jews in a synagogue; and cried entirely too resoundingly in Barcelona's Sagrada Familia. I've even paradoxically joined atheists in group prayer. Some places I've gone only once, others have become places to which I return for spiritual nourishment.

Paul Born, in his book *Deepening Community*, suggests that seeking community is natural, as well as part of the spiritual journey. Instead of viewing communities as places developed for rules and exclusion, Born suggests they are places to share our stories, enjoy one another by spending time together, care for each other, and work to build a better world. Being together satisfies our inherent need to feel cared for and to belong, even if the group isn't always perfectly behaved. Born describes it this way, "Deepening community is the desire to feel safe, knowing that we are part of a community together, that we have our good points and bad and yet are accepted for who we are—yes, at times judged, and yes, at times gossiped about, but never ignored and always included. Deepening community means knowing that, with these people, we belong."

Of course, not all organizations are created equal. Those formed around fear, hate, or a "we will crush that other group" mentality aren't likely to support you in deepening or expanding your personal spirituality. Neither will ones that try to control you, take away your power of choice, or devalue you and your values. Ultimately, it's up to you to find the right fit.

HOW IT WORKS

1. *Close your eyes and visualize* places where you feel spiritually nourished.
2. *Ask yourself* these questions, waiting for an honest answer from within yourself:
    *   How can I deepen my connection to these places?
    *   Would it benefit me to spend more time in these locations?
    *   Is there an opportunity to do seva at any of these sites?
3. *Feel the answers.* Connect with how they feel physically, emotionally, spiritually, and energetically.
4. *Take some breaths.* Inhale and exhale slowly.
5. *Now ask these questions:*
    *   What kind of spiritual spaces am I curious about?
    *   Which of my friend's traditions might be thought-provoking to visit?
    *   Is there anything that holds me back from visiting these places?
6. *Take another breath.* Inhale and exhale slowly.
7. *Write down any ahas* about future actions you might like to take as a result of these reflections.

REBELLIOUS VARIATIONS

If you are seeking a spiritual community: Gather a few friends together for an afternoon of sharing about spiritual journeys. If people mention places that sound intriguing, consider crashing their sacred spaces with them as a host. Or join together to visit a site you've never been before.

Seed a group: Have a lot of meditators in your tribe? Or people who like to watch spiritual movies? Any interest can create something to form a group around.

Virtual can be reality: Technology like Zoom and Skype makes it super easy to gather friends for an afternoon or evening of spiritual moments.

The more the merrier: If you are already part of a spiritual community, look for opportunities to invite others into your community, perhaps by bringing in new topics. My friend Darby Line is active in both a local interfaith group and the Episcopal church. Seeing a chance to deepen her community and build bridges, she invited speakers from other Abrahamic religious traditions to speak at her church, with a Q&A session afterward. She shared with me, "So many congregants told me they had no idea there was so much in common between the faiths. It was incredibly rich and informative. Seeding, expanding, not sure what to call it—for sure opening a lot of eyes and minds."

Start the path: Many of us eventually feel a call to deepen in a particular path, tradition, or religion. That call can challenge us to toss out any baggage we might have accumulated about the R-word: religion, or about our feelings of committing to a group. Yes, it is possible to be spiritual-*and*-religious.

DISCOVER DEEPLY

- Read *How to Be a Perfect Stranger: The Essential Religious Etiquette Handbook* by Stuart M. Matlins and Arthur J. Magida.
- Find road-trip-worthy locations for crashing at atlasobscura.com.

- Read *Moral Tribes: Emotion, Reason, and the Gap Between Us and Them* by Joshua Greene.
- Watch *With One Voice*, which includes mystics from 14 different groups sharing their perspectives.
- Listen to *Deepening Community: Finding Joy Together in Chaotic Times* by Paul Born.
- Read *Whistling Vivaldi: How Stereotypes Affect Us and What We Can Do* by Claude M. Steele.
- Learn about new trends in creating spiritual communities at howwegather.org.

Rebel with (a lot of) clues

* * *

So that's it. You're enlightened now, right? Spiritual AF.*
Living stress-free, consistently full of compassion—even for
your annoying neighbor. Perfectly handling every challenge,
oozing serenity. Your Instagram overfloweth with constant
#instagood inspiration.

Well, maybe some of you are doing all these things. But
most of us are, admittedly, still works in progress. With effort,
our spiritual moments—from Amen to Zen and everything
in between—may be melding into something else: a deeper knowing of ourselves and our sacred connections. As the
Yoga Sūtras of Patañjali suggest, "Any effort toward steadiness
of the mind is spiritual practice." No effort is small. No clue
is meaningless.

True, you may not have done all the activities in this book,
and you may even want to toss a couple of those you did do
into your sacred trash. No worries. The journey is not about
racking up time on a meditation cushion or in a church pew.
Nor is it about chasing the next enlightenment experience,
peak moment, or spiritual high. Instead, it's about living a life
infused with spirit. We are spirituality in progress.

Hopefully, in your journey through this book, you've picked up a few clues about what helps you get—and stay—connected to the sources of spirituality in your life. Returning over and over again to those activities—or dare we now confidently say practices?—can create a strong foundation from which to navigate our lives.

And since you've read this far, permit me to stand on a soapbox for a moment: Being a spiritual rebel does not mean setting ourselves up as superior to people who are involved in *religion*. It's time to stop dumping everything we dislike about *people* onto the word religion. We're simply too smart to sit in denial of where our spiritual practices come from—or conveniently ignore the immense good done by many communities that consider themselves "religious." Instead of throwing the baby out with the proverbial bath water, walking a sacred path necessitates mining the religions and wisdom traditions of the world for their finest bits. Religions—at their best—are groups of caring, spiritual people trying to support each other to get good stuff done in their community (so that all can feel sustained and strengthened). Religions—at their worst—are groups of people focusing on how to keep themselves solid (by excluding those that stretch their ideas of what the community stands for). Spirituality and religion are not opposites. Instead, informing each other, they can be kindred spirits.

It's crucial that our spiritual lives are not about merely chasing joy, serenity, and bliss. In times of stress or loss, our deeper perspective can provide the support we need to deal with the pain we are experiencing inside. Further, it can help us be the life preserver for those around us who are suffering. As we traipse along through our chaotic world—a world brimming with conflict—our spiritual connection can provide much-needed balance and healing. Like the Japanese art of *kintsugi*, where cracks in pottery are mended with powdered gold, we can repair our broken parts not by hiding them, but by shining light into our fractures, honoring them as part of our history, pieces of who we are. Spirituality is the golden glue that holds us together solidly enough to ask the most profound questions.

I AM...

Poet e. e. cummings once said, "It takes courage to grow up and become who you really are." Damn right.
Ask yourself:
- Who am I when no one is looking?
- Who would I be if I had no social media feed, no brand?
- What could happen if I focused less on the opinions of others?

I AM CONNECTED TO...

Now expand.
- Consider when you have felt connected.
- Have you glimpsed anything more expansive than the "*I*ness" of your individuated self?
- How would you describe that connection?

I CONNECT BY...

Consider this Zen saying: "Enlightenment is an accident, and practice makes us accident prone." Take a few moments to review any comments you made in the reflection pages of this book, looking for clues to which spiritual experiences brought you closer to connection.

- What activity would you like to make a more consistent practice?
- What would you like to deepen?
- Were there any activities you didn't have time for, but would want to dip back into?
- What spaces feed your spirituality?
- Which communities feel nurturing and supportive?
- Looking at the next few weeks, how can you expand spiritual moments into your personal spiritual path?

NOTES

* For those of you who just said "Huh?" AF means *to the utmost degree*. Literally, it stands for *as fuck*. Or when I say it: *as Force*.

Revealing higher purpose

* * *

For most of this book, we've been looking at how to deepen our perspective. Now let's tackle higher purpose. Perhaps yours has always been clear to you. My friend Mike once told me that when he was a tot, he thought there was no choice other than firefighter for when he grew up. Not because his father or some other family member fought fires. Nor because he loved fire trucks and the uniform. Nope. It was because on TV he had seen Smokey, a giant brown bear in pants and a hat, tell him it was his responsibility: Remember, only you can prevent forest fires! Mike took that literally. Only he could. No one else. He must become a firefighter. Only he could help.

Childhood symbols often imprint this strongly. For me, of course, it has been the Star Wars universe. Whether it was Leia and the Rebel Alliance trying to save the world from Vader's destructive Death Star, Finn and Rose releasing space horses from their stable prison, or the woke droid L3 demanding equal rights for *all* life forms, I watched those characters seek something greater than their own individual glory.

My sister Amy's childhood inspiration was the courageous Wonder Woman, a damsel who broke free from distress, a powerful symbol of feminine power called to seek justice. Amy's not alone. I recently tossed the following question onto Facebook: Who was your favorite childhood superhero and why? Wonder Woman made the list more than once. So did the Bionic Woman, Catwoman, and sassy Buttercup from the PowerPuff Girls—all for redefining what it means to be female. *X-Men*'s Phoenix, Rogue, and Mystique represented the awesome power of embracing your seeming oddness.

Not surprisingly, masculine energy was represented, too: Batman appeared ("for his dark vibe and lack of traditional superpowers") followed by Superman ("an ordinary person who could do the right thing without needing recognition"). Dropping *super* in favor of epic heroic journeys, people exalted Luke Skywalker (*Star Wars*); Aragorn, son of Arathorn (*Lord of the Rings*); Daenerys Targaryen, Mother of Dragons (*Game of Thrones*); and Katniss Everdeen, the Mockingjay (*The Hunger Games*).

Inspiring characters weren't limited to those in human form. Adorable mutt Benji was admired for knowing what to do in tough situations. Bugs Bunny was appreciated for being smart, resilient, and always a few steps ahead of the game. Serendipitously, a unicorn appeared: Jewel from the *Chronicles of Narnia* series was cited for bravery.

Post after post, people's answers tipped me to what was important to them, what they valued in others, and what traits they most wanted to embody themselves. To up the ante, a few days later I posted a second question: Who is your most inspiring spiritual rebel (dead or alive) and why? Surprisingly, people were even more passionate about their answers. Many infamous personalities appeared, including St. Francis of Assisi, Jesus, the Dalai Lama, Desmond Tutu, and mystic poet Kabir. Modern activists abounded: rebellious Hieronymite nun Sor Juana Inés de la Cruz, secret agent Nancy Wake, the women members of the initiative Roman Catholic Women Priests, Joan of Arc, Chief Joseph, and myriad LGBTQIA+ advocacy groups. Bestselling authors dominated the list, including Alice Walker, Richard Rohr, Madeline L'Engle, Eknath Easwaran, Alan Watts, Matthew Fox, and Anne Lamott. A number of people referenced their personal mentors or the leader of their spiritual community.

And my dear friend Sushmita declared Yoda, perfectly bridging both questions. But the posts were not without controversy: A heated knock-down-drag-out debate about Mother Teresa went on for a few days, proving we're not always aligned about our heroes.

As I read the eloquent, glowing descriptions of just why these people were inspiring, I had an aha! moment that in hindsight seems quite obvious: Both our superheroes and spiritual rebels are *called.* Whether by the bat signal, a deep inner knowing, or divine intervention, the call is one that must be answered.

Likewise, throughout this book, we've sent out calls beyond our unique personalities. Some of us might have heard something coming back or felt something deep within. Others might have seen a glimpse of something. We may have heard our true name. And a few of us might even have heard a calling.

Historically, the word *calling* has described people who felt a pull towards a religious vocation. (In Latin, *vocātiō* means "a call," so that makes sense.) But these days, it's used outside of the religious context, too, taking us past the question: "What do I want to be when I grow up?" It goes beyond whatever Mom, Dad, or some other formative figure whispered to us (or shouted at us) in our childhood. A calling can be discovered through personal yearning and awakening: a meta-purpose, dharma, destiny.

Inspiring vows, creeds, and ethics statements, a calling motivates visioning and planning. Callings are the doing that clothes our being, our spirituality in action. For many of us, our distinct calling is not nearly as epic as it is in comic books, movies, or the sacred texts of our spiritual traditions. Sometimes it lingers just beyond our awareness, waiting for what seems like a lifetime to reveal itself. Often it doesn't show up in our vocation or job, appearing in some other part of our life. Frequently, our calling is just remaining open to opportunities that show up for us, walking through our lives with a constant seva attitude, reflected in everything we do.

During the writing of this book, I was awed (and humbled) by the sheer amount of selflessness going on under the surface of what feels like an increasingly chaotic (and divided) world. Here are just a few examples:

THAT'S THE LAST STRAW

My friend Kelly got me hooked on the anti-straw thing. As I threw a disposable cup away, she nagged (lovingly, of course), "You really should stop using straws." Frankly, I had never thought about it before. Sure, I meticulously snip any six-pack plastic holders into minuscule pieces to keep sea animals safe, but straws were in my blind spot.

After a little research, I learned that Americans throw away 500,000,000 single-use straws a day, which can't be recycled. The Plastic Pollution Coalition informed me that by 2050, our oceans will contain more plastic by weight than fish. Which is gross. Plus, straws and other small plastic items can choke and strangle sea creatures. Which is incredibly sad.

Since the discovery of the infamous floating Great Pacific Garbage Patch, local communities, states, and countries around the world are increasingly banning or taxing single-use plastic, which is a good start. But changing habits based on convenience is not always easy. Lucky for me, through her willingness to smack me lovingly upside the head, Kelly inspired me to finally change my behavior: My backpack now holds a bamboo eating utensil set, a Jedi-logoed water bottle, and my very own fluorescent orange reusable straw.

NO MORE FOR THE ROAD

When it comes to drinking (with or without a straw), Tawny Lara is one of a growing number of people choosing to live #alt-sober. In 2015, she traded in her drunk party girl nights to pursue a different way of living. Starting as an experiment, Tawny decided to stop drinking for a year and, being a writer by trade, to document her journey. On the resulting sobrieteaparty.com site, she sums it up this way, "A booze-free lifestyle (paired with yoga and therapy) has helped me learn who I am and identify the things I was running from." Part personal blog, part podcast, the site is an authentic—and often raw—look into the joys and challenges of living sober in alcohol-soaked New York City. Through sharing openly who she is and what she has experienced, Tawny hopes to inspire others to live "out loud and proud."

As Tawny's sober time grew (way past a single year), so did her desire to help break the stigma of addiction and support others in recovery. So she launched a series of alcohol-free social events including *Readings on Recovery*, which provides a platform for people to share their recovery experience with other like-minded souls, through essays, standup comedy, poetry, live music, and even dance. Intrigued, I tracked her down to learn more. "These events continue to open my eyes," Tawny told me. "Seeing people talk about being in recovery and laughing and smiling reminds me that socializing and being out there is way more important to me than getting fucked up."

Stretching into film, Tawny and her friend B. Rae Perryman, a nationally renowned drug policy advocate who's also in recovery, won the Best Hope Film award at the 2018 New Jersey Recovery Film Festival for their short documentary *Fixed Up*. The film takes a thoughtful look at the proverbial dark side of addiction and light side of recovery, speaking poignantly to the gray areas in between the two.

DON'T ACT BLINDLY, TREAT ANIMALS KINDLY

Until recently, my favorite meme was a cat with a football-helmet-shaped lime on his head, who is affectionately known online as Limecat. The version I have (vintage 2004) was accompanied by this text: "What happens when you: 1) have nothing to do 2) own a sharp knife 3) have a large lime 4) own a patient cat 5) drink too much tequila 6) and it is football season?" I admit the picture was tacked on my fridge for over a decade. Until I met, Karla Kamstra, that is.

Karla, who is one of my heroes, is the founder of Pets Alive in Bloomington, Indiana. The nonprofit spay/neuter and wellness clinic offers low-cost services for pets and helps local shelters keep animals adoptable. Over the last 12 years, Pets Alive has performed over 125,000 surgeries—with only two full-time veterinarians. Their innovative clinic charges a mere $5 for a wellness visit.

One of Karla's leading-edge causes is looking at the intersection of animal welfare issues and internet postings. Animal cruelty is a growing problem online, as some people post videos and pics most of us would agree are disgusting and inhumane.

Many of us are not aware of the animal welfare issues in the seemingly cute videos we repost. Often the animals are drugged or coerced into behavior that is unnatural for them. Or they may be carrying a high level of stress because they don't understand why they are being posed, dressed in strange clothes, or placed in an odd environment. In fact, many amazing wildlife photos are actually staged on game farms where the animals are treated poorly. (Of course, there are some excellent photographers out there actually in nature, but it is getting harder to tell what is fake and what is real, and what might be doing harm to the animals.) There is often a cruel cost for "cute."

In response, Karla is working on an initiative she calls CHIP: Compassionate and Humane Internet Posting. It's not a watchdog group, but a resource to help educate people about compassionate posting and how to recognize signs that an animal is in stress or danger, because there is a difference in the welfare of an animal enjoying itself versus being forced to perform. Karla suggests, "Before you share, like, or comment, look with a discriminating eye. Look through the filter of the animal, and really look at what you're seeing. Does it look like the animal is voluntarily or willingly participating in the antics that you are witnessing? And if not—and you are compassionate to that animal—then don't share it, don't like it."

Which brings me back to Limecat. After talking with Karla, I looked at the meme more carefully, trying to guess the cat's perspective. Result? He is NOT happy. So I took his photo down from my fridge. And I'm a hell of a lot more careful about what I repost now, sticking mostly to pics of my own cats—since I know they are being treated well.

NOT DESERTED IN THE DESERT

Rabbi Daniel Bortz, known as the Millennial Rabbi, and I recently had an animated conversation about Jiu Jitsu, Shabbat, and Coachella—three words that I never would have guessed I'd ever use together in single sentence. Daniel is an avid student of what he calls "Brazilian Jiu [Jew] Jitsu." His tongue-in-cheek play on words is actually a profound comment on mixing traditions within spirituality. He doesn't find the martial art to be out of line at all with his deep Judaism; instead, he finds it deeply nourishing and complementary to his religion. He admits to enjoying breaking the stereotype of what people think of when they think *rabbi* or *Judaism*: "I want to show them there is no box. Yes, there is structure to Judaism, there are things we follow, like kosher and Shabbat, but to me, these are all vehicles for greater meaning. And within that structure, there is so much room for creativity. Anything we do we can learn a lesson from it. Everything you do you can connect to God or elevate the experience."

After becoming a rabbi, Daniel put this idea into action, creating a nonprofit focused on inspiring teens to realize their potential, based on relatable Jewish wisdom. JTEEN of San Diego empowers its members by giving them a voice and a community to explore self-expression—from fun fellowship events like hiking to an entrepreneur program and an award-winning honors knowledge series. JTEENs also learn to extend outside themselves through seva-type activities, such as feeding the homeless and families in need.

Full of creative ideas, Rabbi Daniel then started a Friday night *Shabbat* service that includes breathing and sound therapy. He told me, "I want to tie in the ideas we've had for thousands of years but do so in a more relatable modern way." For those of you asking, "Huh? What's Shabbat?" here's a quick synopsis: Shabbat is a day of rest and celebration that takes place each week starting on Friday evening. And it is awesome. Since in Judaism, days begin at sundown, not at midnight, on Friday evenings, people who practice Shabbat begin celebrating its coming at sunset. Depending on the type of Judaism, people will refrain from certain activities (and do other special things) to honor the day until Saturday's sunset.

Now back to Rabbi Daniel. Since Shabbat is so spiritually nourishing, it's not the kind of thing you want to miss if, for example, you happen to be headed to the Californian desert for Coachella, officially known as the annual Coachella Valley Music and Arts Festival. No worries, you will not be deserted in the desert, because Rabbi Daniel's got you covered. At his Coachella Shabbat Tent, he will hook you up with refreshments, shelter from the sun, *kiddush* and *challah*. If you ask nicely, he might even help you learn a little Jiu Jitsu between music acts.

INCARCERATED IN THE BATHROOM

Darby Christopher recently spent 23 hours confined to her bathroom. After seeing the documentary *Solitary Nation*, she became interested in learning more about challenges in the U.S. prison system. Actually more than interested. Deeply passionate. She recalled, "I can often feel unsure of myself. But with this, I didn't have any feelings of uncertainty at all!"

As she researched, attended conferences, and spoke with others, she increasingly felt called to create a personal sensory experience to give her insight into what solitary confinement might feel like. To raise awareness—and make a difference beyond herself—she asked friends and family to sponsor her for a dollar an hour, with funds going to the National Incarceration Association.

A video she shot just after the bathroom incarceration is surprisingly raw and emotional—even to her. When I spoke with her a few weeks afterwards, I was touched by how deeply the event continued to affect her. Her biggest surprise? How much the lack of good food impacted her. I instantly recalled Maslow's hierarchy of needs: We have needs that must be satisfied for us to survive and thrive, starting with the basics, including food. Darby agreed: "How can we expect people to be better without the basics? It just doesn't make sense."

When I probed her about how this work might support her higher purpose, she offered, "My higher purpose in life is to more and more live out of the Christ space, the Buddha space, Tao. It is being, and then how that being flows out of me into the world. And it sounds so lofty, considering some of my problems, but I claim it!"

ANIMALS FIND SANCTUARY IN A PAW-SOME JAIL

About 800 miles south from Darby, the Stock Island Detention Center in Key West, Florida, is making a difference in the lives of inmates as well as abandoned, abused, and confiscated animals. On an average day, the facility is home to 150 animals and about 600 inmates.

The evolution of the program is almost too peculiar to believe. A group of ducks kept getting hit by cars at a nearby golf course. Since the detention center is built on stilts, the facility coordinated with the sheriff's office to rehome the birds. Of course, word got out, and soon other nearby animal rescue groups followed suit.

Entirely funded by donations (not tax dollars), the sanctuary provides many benefits: homes for needy animals, an opportunity for inmates to be of service, and a channel for much-needed animal welfare outreach, along the lines of: "Kids, don't get a wild pet for your home!"

Yes, you can visit.

DEATH-ROW CHICKENS REJOICE!

In Australia, Julie O'Shea found herself in quite a quandary at an organic animal farm. When she stopped by an organic animal farm to pick up 10 chickens, she ended up rehoming 400 of them, purely by accident—(and with some hard work on social media). When she was told by the farm owner that the "chooks" (Aussie for hens) were going to be culled since they were no longer producing enough eggs for the farmer's liking, Julie immediately reached out to find them new homes through Facebook.

In an interview with the Australian Broadcasting Company's North Coast Bureau, Julie reported that the post had gone viral, with 7,000 views in two days, and she quickly had to develop a system: "I organized a vetting system because I was concerned that people would get them for free and try to on-sell them or take them for their pet snakes or dog baiting. They had to post a picture of their chicken coop and the area where the hens would be." She then met with each rescuer individually.

What's more, this random act of immense compassion awoke something in Julie. Since she had a waitlist from the Facebook post, she's working on making chicken rescue an ongoing project, connecting egg farmers with people to look after their "past-prime" chickens.

SPENDING A BIRTHDAY WITH THE HOMELESS

Sonia Ketchian is a self-professed "love activist," firmly grounded in a higher calling of love: "My work is to help dissolve the illusion of separation which is at the core of the experience of division with inhumanity. To find ways to help diminish human suffering." Instead of throwing a posh party for her 60th birthday, Sonia spent it delivering 60 life-saving backpacks to homeless people in New York City. After emailing friends to enlist help, she was quickly inundated with cases of goods from all over the world. "Everything was just a unity consciousness," she says. "People, I think, want to help other people. If you give them the opportunity, it's pretty amazing what people will do."

The distributed backpacks contained normal things you'd expect, like toiletries and clothing. But they were accompanied by a very unique item. After giving the backpack, Sonia would present each person with a necklace that she and her friends had created, a polished stone heart in a tiny paper bag with the words: *You are loved.* "We would say, 'Well, just in case there's ever a moment where you forget or need to remember, please take this,'" Sonia explains. "And people would just throw their arms around you. It was such a loving experience. It was the best birthday of a lifetime."

Recently, Sonia carried stone love hearts while walking the Camino de Santiago in honor of a loved one who had passed. Handing the hearts to pilgrims she met along the way, she reminded them, "You are loved."

WILL WALK FOR WATER

Speaking of the Camino, my friend Arti Roots Ross recently returned from her trek there. Before leaving the U.S., Arti asked friends to contribute to her charity: water campaign to raise funds and awareness about water issues. She sure educated me. "Many of us have no idea what it's like to be thirsty. We have plenty of water to drink—even the water in our toilets is clean," she told me. "But every day about 1,400 children die from diseases caused by unsafe water and poor sanitation. And it doesn't have to be that way."

In fact, one in 10 people in the world lacks access to clean water. Arti's raised funds will bring water to some of the 663 million people who have no option but to drink dirty water. According to charity:water, clean water not only decreases deaths and improves people's health, but it can also "boost local economies, empower women, and give kids more time in school."

As Arti walked the Camino, she prayed for the healing of the planet and for water to become available to those who need it in the world. Of her experience, she shared with me, "I found myself more and more in relationship with water every day. Not being in a car for five weeks and walking in or near water almost every day shifted my awareness. Some days the Camino asked that we take our shoes off and wade across a beach to the next section of foot trail."

On the road, Arti remembered a friend who would blow a kiss whenever they drove over any kind of bridge or body of water. So on the Camino, she took up that habit, offering a bow of gratitude to each body of water, whatever its size, while taking time to breathe in the immense beauty of the route, honoring it. She also carried the prayers of friends and loved ones, including many for the water, the sea and her creatures, and the beings of the Earth affected by contaminated water. She told me, "The combination kept the awareness of this precious element present with me throughout the pilgrimage journey and even affected my relationship with the frequent rain. I have returned renewed in many ways, strength and resilience restored after a very difficult winter, and a deep gratitude for—and commitment to protecting—clean water for all living creatures in any ways I can."

Arti's story touched me so deeply that I immediately decided to get on the boat, so to speak. For each copy of *Spiritual Rebel* that is sold, I'll make a donation to help some more of those 663 million people without clean water.

* * *

And these stories just scratch the surface of what can happen when we extend what we care about beyond ourselves. Because a higher purpose is limited when it revolves only around our own success. True, studies show that having purpose in our lives gives us direct benefits, including better sleep, healthier behaviors, lower risk of disease, and a longer life. Admittedly, that's cool. But ultimately, *my* higher purpose has very little to do with *me*. And I'm willing to bet *your* higher purpose is more than about just *you*. We can have a tremendous impact on those around us—whether those others are humans, cats, trees, the oceans, or some other piece of Creation.

As our final spiritual experiment together, let's take a moment to reflect on our own stories of higher purpose.

REVEALING HIGHER PURPOSE

Close your eyes, take a few breaths (and a big-ass yawn!). Check in with yourself now. Say these three words slowly: "My higher purpose..."

Is anything coming into view? Did anything develop during your seva experiences that might be a clue? What would be your legacy if the zombie apocalypse wiped us out tomorrow? How might you be a karmic life preserver?

It's unlikely you'll solve *all* of the world's problems in the next few minutes. But you can take the time to remember the importance of purpose in your life and take a quick snapshot of its developing role in your spirituality.

My higher purpose...

The rebel and the saint

Recall how often in human history
the saint and the rebel have been the same person.
ROLLO MAY

* * *

We began this book as spiritual rebels. Courageously stepping into the role of reverent scientists, we excavated, examined, and experimented. As sacred trash inspectors, we clarified our beliefs, tossing out timeworn ones. We journeyed further into wonder and trekked farther into the forest. Embedding spiritual moments of profound being into our daily lives, we mindfully deepened and expanded. Connecting to ourselves and to others, we tapped into something greater than our individuality.

It's not always easy. Life on this planet inherently includes loss, and our paths to deeper perspective and higher purpose may include missteps, trips, falls, and a few bruises. Our spiritual moments can provide a return to balance during those times, provide a better model that makes a life of stress obsolete. I like to call mine *insteads*. Instead of getting drunk after a tough day, I take a trek into the forest. Instead of losing my shit,

I meditate. Instead of a wild shopping spree when I'm feeling less-than, I grab a book and hit some Lectio Divina. Instead of spouting anger at someone on my social feeds, I call a friend to unload. Instead of obsessing about the past or fixating on the future, I can be here now.

Your spiritual journey is likely different from mine. And different from the journeys of everyone you know. We may use different language, engage in different spiritual practices, and hang out in different communities. Yet we are also similar: travelers who are seeking on mystery-filled paths to connect to that God*ish* thing—by whatever words each of us chooses. On this journey, we must not only tolerate each other and "coexist" but also reach out to each other with curiosity. Because our spirituality is most powerful when we are living life connected to each other.

Yes, the Obi-wan of my youth was right: A force flows through us. If we tap it, we can see each other perfectly: We are spiritual rebels *and* rebellious saints.

Always pass on
what you have learned.

YODA

Reflections & Ahas

Reflections & Ahas

Chock full of reflections?
Print your own *Reflections & Ahas Journal*
at spiritual-rebel.com/journal

Pointer words for sacred pondering

* * *

The sacred can show up in infinite forms, including the formless, and through plentiful guides. Below are just a few pointer words to consider:

That Which Makes Trees	The Force	Harold
The Whole	Energy	Life Force
Peace	The Creator	The Something Else
The Hidden	Consciousness	The Way
Higher Power	Tao	Universal Spirit
The Timeless	The Knowing	The One Mind
Great Mystery	Cosmic Consciousness	The Light
The Universe	The All	Divine Nature
The Life Factor	The Divine	All-Providing One
The Unknowable	The Tao	The Relational Energy Field
Wakan Tanka	The Source	Beloved

The All-Pervading	The Invisible	Satnam
Adonai	Higher Force	Goddess
Existence	Being	Supreme Intelligence
Abba	Baba	Great Spirit
The Uncreated	The Eternal	Supreme Being
The Unlimited	Soul Supreme	The Absolute
The Shekinah	Divine Presence	Infinite Intelligence
Brahman	The Witness	Soul Supreme
The Immortal	Granter of Strength	Lord of the Earth
Ultimate Ground of Being	Sacred Spirit	Grandfather
Isha	The Kami	Grandmother
Spirit in the Sky	Shàngdì	Father
Ehyeh	Elyon	Hu
Bahá	All Glorious	Ishwar
Shiva	Vishnu	Shakti
Timeless One	Formless One	Waheguru
Hari	Parvardigar	Heavenly Host
Invisible Creator	The Eternally Awake	Divine Creator
Alpha & Omega	All Sufficient	Author of Life
El Shaddai	The Foundation	Godhead
Holy Spirit	I AM	Kurios
Logos	The Word	Great Shepherd
The First Cause	Higher Mind	First Living Thing
Great High Priest	Righteous One	Sophia
The Unborn One	The One and Only	Shen

Higher Consiousness	The Highest Mind	The Universal Creative Mind
The Self-Knowing One	The Conscious Universe	Self-Knowing Mind of God
Universal Soul	The One Power	Unitary Whole
The Omnipresent	Ultimate Spirit	Olorun
The Blessed	The Truthful	Maheswara
Mother Goddess	Buddha	Timeless Being
Highest Power	Cao Đài	Ancient Immortal
My Refuge	Kyrios	The Firstborn
Great Creator	Spirit	HaShem
Krishna	The Everlasting	The Unconditioned
Jehovah	King of Kings	Lord of Lords
Allah	Eternal Source	The Deity
'ilāhah	Elohim	Yaweh/YHWH
Oludumare	Nonlocal Awareness	Presence
Infinite Void	Unity Consciousness	[x]
Mother Father God	Sovereign One	The One
Bringer of Blessings	Breathmaker	Earthmaker
Mother Earth	Divine Light	Heavenly Mother
Abdullah	The Compassionate One	Living One
Ababinili	God	Androgynous One
Huwa	All Powerful	Ahura Mazda
Dieu	Dios	The Creator
Author of Peace	Heavenly Father	One of Wisdom

Baha	The Immense	The Mediator
Theos	Holy One	The Only
The Divine	Soul of the Universe	Ultimate Source
Christ Consciousness	Nondual Realization	Jesus
Christ	Mary	Beauty
The Still, Small Voice	Creative Source	Divine Flow
Unitive Consciousness	Divine Spark	Love
The Void	The Maker	The All Aware
The Name That Is Beyond Human Knowing		

Sacred shout-outs

* * *

Sean. I adore you. Thanks for monitoring my kite string.

Amy. I love you. And am (still) so sorry about the Putt-Putt pencil.

Fluff Riot. εἴσαστε καταπληκτικοί.

The Frog Coyotes of One Spirit Interfaith Seminary. What an amazing caravan of spiritual rebels! I continue to be inspired by each and every one of you. Everything is (always) holy now.

Monkfish Book Publishing Company. Mere words cannot convey my gratitude to Paul Cohen and my editor Susan Piperato for their brilliant guidance, willingness to cocreate, gentle critiques, ability to polish my hypomanic meandering prose, and for unknowingly manifesting Unifred. Force-full thanks to Colin Rolfe for his stunning and playful book design. Kudos to Dory Mayo and her keen eyes for helping the words show up as perfectly as humanly possible.

The Roxbury. Some writers have cabins or writer's retreats. This rebellious writer is most comfortable (and creative) in the silent, shimmering, sugar-filled sanctuary of the Roxbury Motel. When I arrived to start this book, I received a surprise upgrade to the Angel Hair room. No, not that kind of angel. The glamorous kind that wields an awesome karate punch, a flair for fashion, and a keen sense of crime solving. How auspicious to start this book amongst the kick-ass rebellious women of my childhood. (Plan your trip at theroxburymotel.com.)

The Rose Reading Room at the New York Public Library. Imagine the Sistine Chapel's ceiling. Remove Michelangelo's famous depiction of God and Adam, leaving the entire ceiling full of clouds framed by exquisite layers of complex molding. Fill the room with books and long wooden tables. Now invite anyone who wants to come in—as long as they observe silence. You could say the resulting sacred space might be perfect for writing a book on spirituality. And you'd be right. #librariesrule

And for my father, who art in heaven.*

---

* No, Harold was not his name. Richard was. Because of his love, grace, and ability to withstand my ridiculous (and likely embarrassing) antics, I survived my teens. Through his death, I found my life.

Really recommended reading

* * *

In a world of over 7.7 billion people, 130 million books, and 1.8 billion websites (and growing) there is seemingly no end to the resources available for our spiritual journeys. Here are some of my curated favourites.

PURPOSEFUL BOOKS

The Mystic Heart: Discovering a Universal Spirituality in the World's Religions by Wayne Teasdale

Mindful Paths: Steps Towards a Living Spirituality by Constance McClain and James Walker

The Ten Challenges: Spiritual Lessons from the Ten Commandments for Creating Meaning, Growth, and Richness Every Day of Your Life by Leonard Felder

Twelve Steps to a Compassionate Life by Karen Armstrong

The Art of Happiness at Work by His Holiness the Dalai Lama and Howard C. Cutler, M.D.

Ethics for the Real World: Creating a Personal Code to Guide Decisions in Work and Life by Ronald A. Howard and Clinton D. Korver

Good Citizens: Creating Enlightened Society by Thich Nhat Hanh

The Book of Forgiving: The Fourfold Path for Healing Ourselves and Our World by Desmond Tutu and Mpho Tutu

The Life You Can Save: How to Do Your Part to End World Poverty by Peter Singer

A Plea for the Animals: The Moral, Philosophical, and Evolutionary Imperative to Treat All Beings with Compassion by Matthieu Ricard

GreenFaith: Mobilizing God's People to Save the Earth by Fletcher Harper

INSPIRING WEBSITES

Charter for Compassion: charterforcompassion.org

Unity Earth: unity.earth

The Fetzer Institute: fetzer.org

Parliament of the World's Religions: parliamentofreligions.org

Spirituality & Health: spiritualityhealth.com

Parabola: parabola.org

Lion's Roar: lionsroar.com

The Christian Century: christiancentury.org

Tikkun: tikkun.org

The Chopra Center: chopra.com

One Spirit Interfaith Seminary: onespiritinterfaith.org

Omega Institute for Holistic Studies: eomega.org

Kripalu Center for Yoga & Health: kripalu.org

THOUGHT-PROVOKING PODCASTS

On Being: onbeing.org

BBC Heart and Soul: bbc.co.uk/programmes

Harry Potter & The Sacred Text: harrypottersacredtext.com

Tarot for the Wild Soul: lindsaymack.com/podcast
Beneath the Surface: rabbibortz.com/podcast
Chai & Chat: krishnadas.com/category/podcasts
The Liturgists: theliturgists.com/the-liturgists-podcast
The RobCast: robbell.com/portfolio/robcast

REMARKABLE RECOVERY RESOURCES

Sober Curious: The Blissful Sleep, Greater Focus, Limitless Presence, and Deep Connection Awaiting Us All on the Other Side of Alcohol by Ruby Warrington

Breathing Under Water: Spirituality and the Twelve Steps by Richard Rohr

The 12-Step Buddhist: Enhance Recovery from Any Addiction by Darren Littlejohn

Recovery—The Sacred Art: The Twelve Steps as Spiritual Practice (The Art of Spiritual Living) by Rabbi Rami Shapiro and Joan Borysenko Ph.D.

From Survival to Recovery: Growing Up in an Alcoholic Home by Al-Anon Family Groups

Dry: A Memoir by Augusten Burroughs

Wishful Drinking by Carrie Fisher

Lit: A Memoir (P.S.) by Mary Karr

The Dark Side of The Light Chasers by Debbie Ford

... plus a robust list of websites at spiritual-rebel.com/recovery

Sarah Bowen **is a multifaith spiritual educator and speaker, and an aspiring Jedi.**

As a member of One Spirit Interfaith Seminary's faculty, Spiritual Directors International, and several recovery communities, she seeks to help others connect with the higher power of their own understanding. Passionate about the world's great faith traditions, Sarah is a graduate of One Spirit and has studied at Chicago Theological Seminary, Emerson Theological Institute, Chopra Center, and Omega Institute. She is especially interested in the intersection of animal welfare and spiritual values. A fierce advocate for all creatures, Sarah currently serves as an animal chaplain.

Before starting her spiritual journey, Sarah spent a few decades as a designer and brand strategist in New York City. Her first book, *Void If Detached: Seeking Modern Spirituality Through My Father's Old Sermons* (Epigraph Publishing, 2017), has received several awards.

Sarah splits her time between New York City's Hell's Kitchen and the Hudson Valley, where she lives with her artist husband Sean Bowen, two rebellious black cats named Deacon and Buba-ji, Picasso the rescued goldfish, Max the squirrel, and a backyard full of yet-to-be-named critters.

Connect at thisissarahbowen.com
or follow her on Instagram @modernreverend